Motorbooks International
WARBIRD HISTORY

MiG-15

N15MG

Yefim Gordon and Vladimir Rigmant

First published in 1993 by Motorbooks International Publishers & Wholesalers, PO Box 2, 729 Prospect Avenue, Osceola, WI 54020 USA

Motorbooks International books are also available at discounts in bulk quantity for industrial or sales-promotional use. For details write to Special Sales Manager at the Publisher's address

Library of Congress Cataloging-in-Publication Data
    Gordon, Yefim.
        MiG-15/Yefim Gordon, Vladimir
        Rigmant.
            p. cm. – – (Warbird history series)
        Includes index.
        ISBN 0-87938-793-9
        1. MiG-15 (Jet fighter plane) I. Rigmant,
        Vladimir. II. Title. III. Series.
    UG1242.F5G64   1993
    623.7'46044– –dc20   93-1159

Printed and bound in Hong Kong

On the front cover: A former Chinese Navy MiG-15bis restored by Unlimited Aircraft Ltd. *Michael O'Leary*

On the back cover: A drawing that shows the MiG-15 in Hungarian, Cuban, American, and movie markings (more details inside).

On the frontispiece: A former Chinese Navy MiG-15bis. *Michael O'Leary*

On the title page: The MiG-15 and its former nemesis, the F-86 Sabre, are now available for purchase on the open market. These two jets, formerly owned by the Combat Jets Flying Museum, are now part of the EAA collection. *Michael O'Leary*

Contents

Acknowledgments

This book is a result of joint efforts of Motorbooks International and Moscow-based AviaData. Initiating this book project, which is one of the first in a string of AviaData produced books on aviation history, we have set a goal of providing better knowledge and understanding of Russian aircraft and Air Force history for Western readers.

I would like to express my deepest gratitude to all the people who assisted with this multinational project: Greg Field, Motorbooks International Aviation Editor; Yefim Gordon, "motor" of many AviaData book projects, and his co-author Vladimir Rigmant; numerous contributors who supplied valuable materials for the book; and the Russian fighter pilots who fought in Korea and shared their genuine, first-hand experience.

A special thanks to the team of AviaData translators: Raisa Shuyanova, who carried the major load of translating this book into English; Yuri Dimidov and his friends responsible for the technical translation; Vladimir Sazonkin, who acted both as translator and editor for AviaData; and Alexy Zakharov, who worked on both Russian and English language versions of the book. Personal thanks to Valentin Vetlitsky, who made all graphics and color illustrations for this book, and to Irina Minaeva and Varvara "Varya" Mikhailova, who typed innumerable pages of Russian and English language versions of the book.

Finally, we wish to thank noted aviation writer Robert F. Dorr for valuable editorial assistance.

Boris B. Rybak
AviaData Director

The aim of this book, written by Russian authors, is not only to describe a history of development of the MiG-15 and its numerous derivatives but to present for the first time the point of view of the Russian fighter pilots who flew combat missions in the Korean War. The authors chose not to question or embellish the pilots' reminiscences, choosing instead to present their stories, along with the latest historical facts and photographs from the Russian military archives.

We would like to thank the following persons for their contributions: Victor Drushlykov, Waclaw Holys, Victor Kabanov, Dmitry Khazanov, Konstantin Kosminov, David Oliver, Gennady Petrov, Vladimir Sazonkin, Issaak Spivak, Ivnamin Sultanov, Valentin Vetlitsky, Alexy Zakharov, and Steven Zaloga. Special thanks to Russian pilots, veterans of the war in Korea: Boris Abakumov, Sergey Kramarenko, Georgy Lobov, Eugeny Pepelyaev, Georgy Okhai, Nikolay Shkoda, Nikolay Zameskin.

Yefim Gordon
Vladimir Rigmant

Introduction

When the MiG-15 appeared in Korean skies, it shocked and stunned most Americans who had never thought that an enemy might possess the edge in battle and who had never, in their history, known defeat. Only those of us who lived through that era can understand the awe we felt toward the MiG-15. To Americans who flew against it in the North American F-86 Sabre, suffered frustrations and defeats, and in the end prevailed over the MiG-15, the Soviet fighter was a deadly opponent. These Americans knew that some of the MiGs coming aloft from Chinese bases were being flown by Russians. Until publication of this volume, we never realized quite how many Russians—and how soon they really joined the battle.

This book marks a turning point in the West. Never before has a complete history appeared of the design, development, and operational and combat use of the MiG-15. In this volume, for the first time, readers in the West will learn how the Soviet Union deployed its pilots and aircraft to Korea, how they planned their campaign against Allied air forces, and even the untold story of how they captured an F-86. Only in this post-Cold War era can this story from the Soviet viewpoint finally be told.

These first-person stories by Soviet officers ring with authenticity. Like real life—and like reminiscences by American pilots—they are inconsistent. One pilot tells us in a frank and very human way of weaknesses of the Soviet system while reaffirming his loyalty to it. Another gives us stiff and steadfast Cold War rhetoric, accusing Americans in Korea of terror attacks against the civilian populace. One pilot recalls that friends, family, and even outsiders in his home town knew of the Soviet role in Korea, while another insists that "participation of the Soviet Air Force in this war was secret and concealed from Soviet citizens." Yet when these men speak of events previously unknown in the West, such as the Russian capture of an F-86 Sabre, the differing musings of different men reinforce each other.

To set personal remembrances in context, this volume contains editorial notes that were added to point out important discrepancies between the Russian viewpoint and American records.

The MiG-15. It's a story that waited more than forty years to be told and now it's here, straight from the Russians who flew and fought.

Robert F. Dorr
Oakton, Virginia

Chapter 1

I-310—The MiG-15 Prototype

During the Great Patriotic War (the Soviet name for the Second World War), dramatic changes in aircraft design came quickly. The piston engine exhausted its prospects for further development. The first jet engines appeared. Production and operation of jet aircraft began. The first flights were made of prototype and production aircraft powered by jet engines. Jets saw combat.

During the war, progress that might have taken decades was crammed into just a few short years.

In postwar years, achievements in aerodynamics, engine design, and manufacturing produced a number of swept-wing jet aircraft. The first jets naturally were fighters. Those that entered service in 1945–1952, capable of near-sonic speeds of 560–745mph (900–1,200km/h) with swept or thin straight wings, are known to Russians as "First Generation" fighters.

The MiG-15 and F-86 fighters are the most successful and popular First Generation aircraft. Both flew for the first time in 1947, went through similar development stages, and served operationally in their own countries and those of allies.

The F-86 and MiG-15 were more or less equivalent in flight performance. They had some differences in configuration as well as in avionics, equipment, and armament packages. Air combat between the two was especially deserving of attention when they were flown by pilots worthy of each other.

The MiG-15 was destined for a long service life. It was built in great quantity, in many versions, and even today one can see it at airfields in many countries.

Soviet aircraft have been developed under conditions of super-secrecy. For this reason, myths have taken hold concerning creation of the MiG-15.

Myth number one: the MiG-15 was not a new aircraft but an in-depth modification of the Focke-Wulf Ta-183, developed by Kurt Tank.

Myth number two, which arose as a consequence of the first: Soviet aircraft designers could not do something worthwhile, and the MiG-15 would never have appeared without use of captured German material and "captive brains."

The use of the captured materials in developing advanced technologies was not an unusual practice, and the USSR was not alone in doing this. The United States, Great Britain, and other countries took advantage of German projects after the war.

By the end of the war, the Soviet aircraft industry was fully capable of developing and producing jet aircraft on its own. Undisputedly, the USSR could have quickly created powerful turbojets and transonic fighters without resorting to foreign prototypes or "trophy" aircraft, but Soviet designers had a very short time (months, sometimes only days) because of the pressures of the Cold War. Under the J. Stalin regime, no one joked about harsh reality: in the race for technology, the lives of designers were at stake. The cost of failure was very high. This is why Soviet designers sometimes preferred not to take risk but use foreign technical solutions.

The capabilities of the MiG-15 were derived from what Russians called three "whales," or ground rules: a turbojet delivering over 4,410lb (2,000kg) thrust; a new configuration with swept wing and empennage; introduction of new pilot survival aids, including ejection seat. These, together with powerful armament and ease of manufacture and operation, allowed Soviet designers to create a superb technical product in the MiG-15.

Engine Development

Turbojet development in the USSR began in the early 1920s. In 1923, the world's first aircraft turboprop engine layout, suggested by V. Bazarov, received a patent.

In 1926 at the Nauchno-Issledovatelsky Avtomotorny Institut (NAMI; Scientific Research Automotive Engine Institute), a special design group was organized under N. Brilling to work on turbine engine research. The main focus of this group was the turboprop engine. After 1930, this group was headed by V. Uvarov, a famous scientist and engineer in the field of turbine engine design. The Uvarov design group designed the 1,150hp GTU-3 turboprop engine for A. Tupolev's TB-3 bomber in 1936. Two engines were built and passed through intensive tests in 1938–1940, but the TB-3 flew with piston engines only.

A second step in turbojet engine development in the USSR was creation of the A. Lyulka turbojet at Kcharkov Aviation Institute. This first Soviet turbojet was designated RD-1. Rated at 1,105lb (500kg) thrust, this engine was 75 percent ready when the Great Patriotic War began. The Uvarov group also developed a 4,410lb (2,000kg) thrust engine.

The war with Germany interrupted turbojet development work in the USSR. Work on turbojet designs resumed in 1944, when the outcome of the war

A British Nene-1 turbojet engine on a test bench in the Soviet Union.

could be foreseen, and it appeared possible to divert some efforts to development of new, advanced engines and aircraft. A. Lyulka continued his work on turbojet design, which resulted in the prototype T-1 turbojet delivering 2,866lb (1,300kg) thrust. Shortly afterward, the A. Mikulin OKB (design bureau) also started work on a turbojet design.

By then, jet engines and aircraft were in production in the West. The USSR risked falling far behind. To save time, approval was given to the only realistic decision—to launch series production of German Jumo-004 and BMW-003 turbojets, which had centrifugal-flow compressors, thrust ratings of 1,984lb (900kg) and 1,763lb (800kg), and Soviet designations RD-10 and RD-20 respectively.

These turbojets, and the Yak-15 and MiG-9 prototypes they powered, gave Soviet industry its first acquaintance with jet technology. At the same time, it was decided to buy the most advanced Western Nene and Derwent turbojets with centrifugal-flow compressors and to introduce them into production in the USSR.

Soviet engine designers needed two to three more years for prototype and full scale development of newer, more powerful axial-flow turbojets. This time was used effectively: by the 1950s, a number of turbojets with thrust ratings of 6,613lb–20,645lb (3,000–9,000kg) were in production. All were based on the indigenous Soviet prototypes.

As the Cold War began, M. Khrunichev, the Soviet Aircraft Industry Minister, accompanied by designer A. Yakovlev, reported to J. Stalin on their intention to buy state-of-the-art British Nene and Derwent turbojets. "Uncle Joe" with the immediacy peculiar to him, asked, "What fool will sell us his secret?" But it was 1946, Soviet-Western relations were still cordial, and Stalin's "fools" abounded at Rolls-Royce and in the British Labor Government.

A. Mikoyan , aircraft designer, V. Klimov, engine designer, and S. Kishkin, metallurgical engineer, were sent to England to negotiate acquisition of the turbojets. They acquired 30 Derwent-5 and 25 Nene-1 and Nene-2 engines, which were attentively studied at the Central Institute of Aviation Motors (TsIAM). Flight testing with a Tupolev Tu-2 twin-engine bomber test bed, designated Tu-2LL, was initiated.

Nene-1 engines were tested on the Tupolev "72" and "73" aircraft and were chosen for the "73" prototype (later well known as the Tu-14 bomber). The Derwent-5 was considered a fighter engine and was used in Yakovlev and Lavochkin OKB projects.

At the same time production of the British turbojets began at Soviet engine plants. The Derwent-5 was introduced in production under the Soviet designation RD-500. The Nene-1 was coded RD-45 and the Nene-2, RD-45F. The numbers *500* and *45* corresponded with numbers of the plants where they were produced. V. Klimov was head of production and was also busy modernizing and further developing these turbojets.

During 1947–1948, Soviet fighters such as the Yak-23, Yak-30, and La-15 made their maiden flights, powered by the 3,505lb (1,590kg) thrust RD-500. The RD-45 was heavier and was intended for the Tu-14 and Il-28 bombers.

In choosing the RD-45 for its new fighter, the Mikoyan OKB took some risk, as it had done in 1939 when developing the MiG-1. It worked. The Mikoyan I-310 prototype with Nene-1, later designated MiG-15 with RD-45 and RD-45F, became the main Soviet fighter. Although Yakovlev fighters were more maneuverable, the MiG could fly faster and its armament was more lethal.

Early RD-45s and RD-45Fs had a short service life—only hundred of hours and less than the prototype—because Soviet designers used indigenous materials of poor quality. Later, Soviet designers developed the RD-45FA using new materials and structural improvements. Service life was doubled.

The Klimov OKB used RD-500 and RD-45 experience and TsIAM research into centrifugal compressors to create more powerful and cost-efficient centrifugal-flow turbojets. In 1949, the VK-1 turbojet emerged. It was a further development of the RD-45 with 5,952lb (2,700kg) thrust. When the VK-1 was equipped with afterburner, the resulting VK-1F delivered 7,451lb (3,380kg) thrust with afterburning. Structural and manufacturing improvements then produced the VK-1A version, with service life increased to 150-200hr.

In due course, the VK-1 engine gave new life to the MiG-15bis, the advanced version of the MiG-15. The engine also powered Il-28 tactical bombers and Tu-14T torpedo bombers.

Western countries also relied heavily on the Nene and later Rolls-Royce engines to power their first jets. In 1947, Pratt & Whitney began producing the Nene-2 under licence from Rolls-Royce. The early F9F Panther was powered by a Nene, designated J42. A later version of the Nene became the J48, called the Tay in England. The J48 was capable of 7,275lb (3,300kg) thrust dry and 8,377lb (3,800kg) with afterburning. The French engine-maker Hispano-Suiza obtained licence to build the Nene in 1946 and modernized it repeatedly over the following eight years. Hispano-Suiza also manufactured a Tay variant delivering 6,285lb (2,850kg) thrust. This maker's best production turbojet, the Verdon, was developed from the Tay and attained a dry thrust rating of 7,716lb (3,500kg), raised to 9,920lb (4,500kg) with afterburning. These engines powered Dassault Mystere fighters in successive versions, but comparably advanced development of the Nene was bypassed in the USSR.

The centrifugal-flow turbojet proved more serviceable than early axial-flow turbojets. However, as speeds increased, centrifugal-flow powerplants proved no longer fuel-efficient. Higher speeds required greater thrust and, hence, greater airflow. A centrifugal-flow engine offered less thrust than an axial-flow engine having the same frontal area. Further, the centrifugal-flow turbojet was limited by its single stage compression ratio of 4.2–4.4. Since multi-stage versions were not developed, the centrifugal-flow turbojet reached its peak of development with thrust ratings of 6,613–8,818lb (3,000–4,000kg) between the end of the Great Patriotic War and the early 1950s.

Jet-Airframe Design

Early jet aircraft were configured just about the same as piston-engine planes. While turbojets were being improved, however, it became clear that changes had to be made in a typical airplane's aerodynamic shape and general design.

As is well known, a principal challenge in aircraft design is to obtain the correct c.g. (center of gravity). For conventional designs, c.g. must be located at one-third to one-fourth of wing mean aerodynamic chord. With a piston engine, this meant positioning the engine at the front of the aircraft, ahead of the c.g. and the wing. Fuel was in the c.g. zone, and the crew behind it. The weight of propeller and engine was balanced by the weight of the rear fuselage and empennage.

If a turbojet were mounted in the nose of an aircraft, exhaust gases would have to be directed downward, under the fuselage. Placing engines on the wing sidestepped this problem, and this is how

the German He-280, Me-262, British Gloster Meteor and Soviet Su-9 and I-211/215 (designed by S. Alekseev) fighters were configured.

Early Soviet jet fighters were created hurriedly. Designers selected configurations identical to those of piston-engine aircraft, with engine up front and exhaust directed downward. This configuration was called "Redan" in Russia. The Yak-15 was simply a jet version of the propeller-driven Yak-3. Its only change was its Jumo-004 (RD-10) turbojet, installed instead of a VK-105PF piston engine in the nose and slightly below in order to direct exhaust gases under the fuselage.

Since turbojets were lighter than piston engines, the pilot and some internal loads could be moved forward; this also improved the pilot's forward and downward visibility. Since there was no propeller, the height of landing gear could be reduced. Tricycle landing gear avoided any need to locate a tail wheel in the jet exhaust. This Redan configuration was not a Soviet invention, having been employed on the German Messerschmitt P.1101, P.1106, and Heinkel P.1078, but all Soviet postwar jet fighters had it. These were the Yak-15, Yak-17, Yak-23, MiG-9, La-150, La-152, La-156, and La-174TK.

In the West, the Redan-style configuration was not widely used. Among early jet fighters, only the Swedish Saab J29 Tunnan (Barrel) had such a layout, even though this configuration was efficient.

There was another variation, with the engine mounted over the fuselage. Even though this freed up fuselage space for pilot, load, and fuel, this design was impractical due to high engine nacelle drag and the problem of an emergency escape

arrangement for the pilot. Only two aircraft were actually built with this configuration, the prototype Fieseler Fi-103 (manned version of the V-1 "buzz bomb") and production He-162.

As a logical next step in jet fighter development, the relatively light turbojet was moved backward, the cockpit forward. Because the length of a typical engine now decreased, it could be moved back so that its exhaust coincided with the empennage. The forward fuselage could then extend farther ahead of the wing.

Once the turbojet was moved backward, there appeared two air intake types: nose and lateral inlets. Both types of intakes had advantages and shortcomings. A nose intake made it necessary to increase nose and mid-fuselage cross section area. Lateral intakes made it necessary to increase fuselage width in front of the wing. With the appearance of powerful and bulky radars, the issue of air-intake arrangement was settled because the radar would have to be placed in the nose, making nose intakes impractical.

Swept Wings

By the end of the Great Patriotic War, pilots who flew high-performance piston fighters such as the P-51 Mustang would sometimes approach sonic speed in a dive. In such a dive the controls became increasingly difficult to move as speed increased: the nose would try to tuck under, and sometimes the controls would reverse. It took enormous effort by a pilot to recover from this dangerous mode.

With jet aircraft, level flight speeds increased into the sonic range. Shock effects, which pilots prop-driven aircraft

RD-45F and VK-1A Specifications

	RD-45F (Nene-2)	VK-1A
Maximum static thrust	5,005lb (2,270kg)	5,953lb (2,700kg)
rpm	12,300	11,560
Dry weight	1,562–1,602lb (703–726kg)	1,952lb (884.5kg)*
Diameter	4ft (1.25m)	4ft 2in (12.73m)
Length	5ft 4in (2.45m)	5ft 5in (2.57m)*
Specific fuel consumption	1.065	1.07**

*without jet pipe
**at maximum thrust

had encountered briefly, now became routine. At times, uncontrollable aircraft dove into the ground burying not just pilots, but the secrets of transonic flight. In-depth study of transonic aerodynamics was needed.

Wind tunnel tests showed that a thin symmetrical wing section and swept wings could resolve this "shock-wave crisis."

In 1935, Dr. A. Busemann, German aerodynamicist, first reported on the swept-wing concept. During the war, he continued his investigations, and the Germans used a 30–35deg swept wing on several of their aircraft. The Me-262, He-162, and Ta-183 (which looked somewhat like the future MiG-15) fighters were ready by the end of the war.

The main peculiarity of the swept wing was that airflow was divided into two components. The first flew past the wing to the quarter-chord line, and the second spanwise. The spanwise component caused boundary layer movement to the wing tip, causing the wing's tip to stall. The spanwise flow also made the wing control surfaces less efficient. To prevent this loss of efficiency, many Soviet aircraft were equipped with fences on the upper wing surface. These fences caused vortexes to form, hampering boundary layer overflow and early separation.

In the USSR, the idea of the swept wing was devised by V. Struminsky in 1946 at the Tsentralny Aerogidrodinamichesky Institut (TsAGI; Central Aerohydrodynamics Institute). Struminsky, G. Byushgens, and other scientists conducted research on swept-wing flow laws. Basic concepts for swept-wing aircraft stability and controllability analysis were created.

The TsAGI embarked on a major pro-

The Mikoyan-Gurevich I-310 was the prototype for the MiG-15. This aircraft is S-01, the first of three I-310s produced. Construction on the aircraft began in the spring of 1947, and it first flew on 30 December 1947. It is shown here during Mikoyan development tests.

The first I-310 was much like the future MiG-15, except that it lacked air-brake panels on the rear fuselage. It carried two 23mm cannons on the left and a single 37mm cannon on the right.

gram to study a 35deg swept wing. This was exactly the wing later recommended for the Lavochkin La-160 and Mikoyan I-310 (MiG-15 prototype).

Swept wings were tested experimentally on flying models dropped from a Tupolev Tu-2 prop-driven bomber. During 1945–1948, working for Letno-Issledovatelsky Institut (LII; Flight Test Research Institute of Ministry of Aircraft Industry), P. Tsybin created the LL-1 and LL-2 gliders. These were intended for speed tests at about 718mph (1,150km/h) and were used as flying laboratories to study transonic aerodynamics. These powder rocket-boosted gliders with water ballast were towed to a prescribed altitude, from which they were dropped with their booster operating for maximum speed. The experiment was conducted while diving, after which the pilot recovered, released water ballast, and landed. The LL-1 glider had a straight wing, the LL-2 a forward-swept wing. The LL-3, which was not built, was to have had a 30deg swept-back wing.

At the end of the Great Patriotic War, German aircraft designers in Soviet-occupied territory were deported to the USSR to develop new-generation aircraft. In the Podberezye settlement, near the town of Dubna, two new OKBs were organized. One was headed by B. Baade and G. Ressing. Soviet specialists P. Obrubov and A. Bereznyak were appointed as their deputies. This OKB continued work on the German DFS-346 design, which was practically ready. This aircraft, with the Soviet designation 346, was transported in 1946 to TsAGI for full-scale aerodynamic tests inside the T-101 wind tunnel.

The 346 was an all-metal, mid-wing monoplane. Its fuselage was composed of three subsections—nose, cylindrical center fuselage, and lower fuselage with a retractable ski installed. The pressurized cockpit was in the nose. The pilot lay prone, face down. This cockpit was detachable, with an escape unit that ejected the pilot after it was detached. The airplane's Walther liquid-fuel rocket engine provided 8,818lb (4,000kg) thrust. Total fuel and oxidizer capacity was 4,188lb (1,900kg). This capacity permitted engine operation of up to 2min. The aircraft could accelerate up to about Mach 2.0.

In 1947–1948, LII test pilots Sultan Amet-Khan, S. Anokhin, and N. Rybko conducted more than 100 flight tests and received comparative experimental data

on two wing types. At the same time, work continued on the Bisnovat B-5 and on the 346, both with a 45deg swept wing.

In 1948, flight tests began on the 346 with an inoperative engine. The first powered flight was in 1949. In its first flight, the aircraft was dropped from one of three B-29s interned by the Soviets in the Far East. It accelerated quickly and began a vertical climb. Then the pilot radioed that it was out of control. Its cockpit detached and the pilot ejected safely. This was not merely the first but the last 346 flight.

The B-5 aircraft was developed under M. Bisnovat and was intended for transonic speed research. This aircraft was powered by an L. Dushkin liquid-propellant rocket engine. Test flights began in 1948. The B-5 was dropped from a Petlyakov Pe-8 bomber. Two of these aircraft made a total of nearly ten flights.

Development of the 346 and B-5 acquainted designers with a 45deg swept wing. Meanwhile, a 35deg swept wing, in theory already validated, was installed on the Lavochkin La-160 Strelka (Arrow) prototype. The aircraft was developed from earlier S. Lavochkin fighter proto-

The first I-310 prototype was powered by a British-made Nene-1 turbojet delivering 4,928lb (2,230kg) thrust. The high-set tailplane became traditional for Soviet fighters of the late 1940s.

types. It differed from previous Lavochkins in having a swept wing with a thin airfoil. Flight trials held June–September 1947 tested its stability and control characteristics. The La-160 was further developed while being tested: fences were fitted to the top surface of the wing. Installation of fences became standard for Soviet designers: the greater the wing sweep angle, the larger the number of stall fences. The La-160 reached 652mph (1,050km/h), or Mach 0.92, in a dive. At the same time, Lavochkin tested the La-174TK with a thin, straight wing and more powerful Derwent engine. In spite of the extra power, the La-174TK was slower than the swept-wing La-160, proving the superiority of swept wings for high-speed aircraft.

Gradually, experience with swept wing was built up. This experience was applied successfully to the MiG-15, La-15, and Yak-30 fighters.

Like the production MiG-15 that followed, the I-310 packed a heavier punch than American fighters of the era. Shown here is the 37mm cannon on the right side.

Ejection Seats

In jet aircraft capable of transonic speeds, conventional escape methods became impossible. New methods, such as ejection, were needed.

The first attempts to make bailout easier were undertaken in the late 1920s and early 1930s in Germany, but these ended at the ground-test stage. Ejection systems were used for the first time during the Great Patriotic War in German high-speed piston and turbojet aircraft. Two ejection systems were developed in Germany, a cartridge system and one using compressed air, either of which actuated a piston in a special tube behind the pilot's seat.

The cartridge ejection system was used by Heinkel in the He-162 fighter, which had its engine atop the fuselage. The cartridge had a metal, 1in (28mm) diameter shell of 3in (75mm) length, a smokeless powder charge weighing 1.2oz (34g), and a 0.14oz (4g) black powder fuse. In an emergency, the pilot put his leg on footrests, jettisoned his canopy, and pulled an ejection lever.

Ejection time at a maximum G-load of 11.5 was 0.178 second. Ejection speed was 42.63ft/sec (13.2m/sec). Advantages of the cartridge ejection system included low weight and structural simplicity. Dependence on the powder charge was a shortcoming.

The compressed air ejection system was used on the He-280 jet and He-219 two-seat, piston-engine fighters. This system was more weighty and complex and required air bottles, a fast-acting valve, and plumbing. Weight of the He-219 ejection seat was 61lb (27.9kg), or 16.3lb (7.4kg) more than that of the He-162's seat.

After the war, the work of German designers was of great interest to the Allies. Many German documents and prototypes were captured by the British, and much analysis of German work was conducted in the USSR and the United States.

Soviet attempts to design an ejection seat date to 1940. In the course of new fighter development, designers I. Florov and A. Borovkov addressed the problem of pilot survival at speeds of 330–530mph (528–850km/h) and altitudes up to 20,000ft (6,000m). Their aircraft configuration was similar to the Saab J21 with a pusher propeller and ramjet boosters. Their escape device, which would turn the seat with the pilot and eject it downwards via pneumatic springs, was proposed for this project. The war interrupted the development of this fighter, hence, of the first Soviet ejection system.

It was not until after the war when work on a Soviet ejection seat resumed. The Mikoyan OKB, teamed with TsAGI, LII, and the Aeromedicine Institute, became a leader in ejection-seat development. Tests were performed at LII's facilities. A device was constructed with a cart that moved along a long vertical guiderail, was accelerated by an explosive charge, and then slowed by powerful brakes. LII engineers determined the size of the charge to get the required G-load. After tests with dummies and animals, it was decided to carry out the first manned test. Six strong men were ejected from the cart with at the G-load up to the maximum.

Next came flight tests. These began cautiously, using a dummy for the first aerial ejections. A Pe-2 bomber was used; its twin tail made it ideal for ejection trials. The seat was installed on a guiderail in the gunner's slot behind the pilot. Initially, the seat was not stabilized (it simply tumbled around). Ejection sequence and seat path were recorded by a camera aboard the Pe-2. The seat was modified based on motion-picture analysis and by July 1947 manned tests could begin.

G. Kondrashov, a veteran parachutist and pilot, was chosen. He had made more than 700 parachute jumps. On 24 July 1947, Kondrashov successfully performed the first ejection in the USSR.

The first ejection seat was of cartridge-fired design. The ejection unit and the seat pan were attached to the frame. The pilot sat on his parachute, which lay in the seat pan. A static line spring hook

Top to bottom: the first I-310 (S-01) prototype without fuselage-mounted air-brake panels and GSAP camera; the second prototype, S-02, equipped with anti-spin rockets installed under the wings; the third prototype, S-03, was equipped the RPKO-10 compass; the production MiG-15 (SV) equipped with RV-2 radio altimeter, NR-23 guns, and external fuel tanks of 66gal (250ltr) capacity each: the production MiG-15 (S) with underwing external fuel tanks of 106gal (400ltr) capacity each; the MiG-15 (SU) fighter prototype with vertically flexible gun mount.

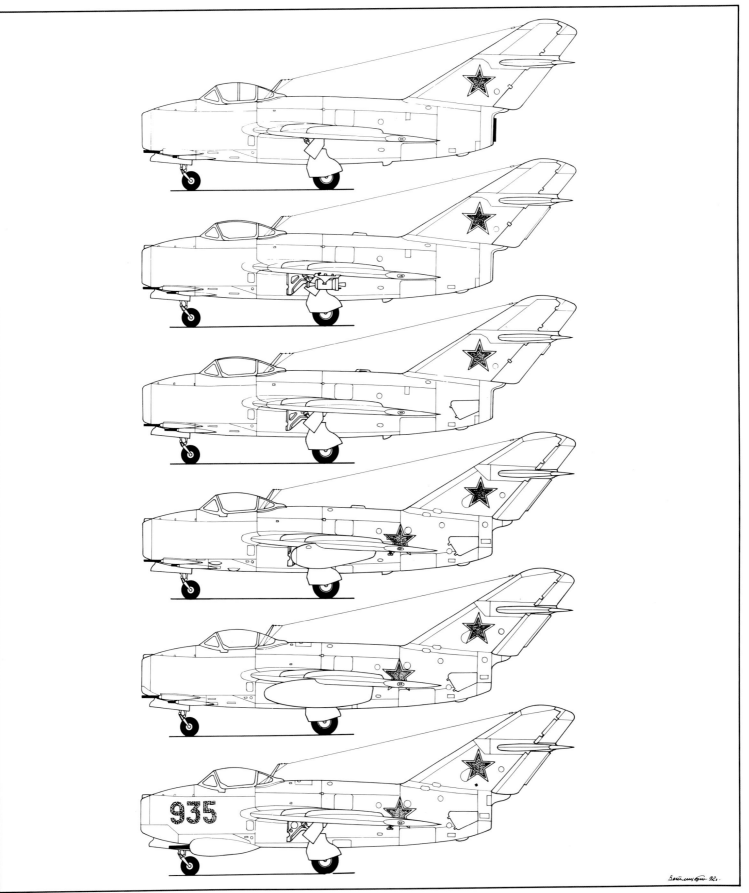

The second I-310 fighter, designated S-02, first flew on 27 May 1948. S-02 was equipped with a British Nene-2 engine, had a more complete avionics suite, increased aileron area, and an ASP-1N optical gun sight. Because S-02 was used for spin testing, the aircraft was equipped with an anti-spin rocket under each wing.

was attached. After ejection, the pilot had to push the seat away. Only then, the parachute opened.

The minimum safe altitude for an ejection was 656–984ft (200–300m). At speeds over 435mph (700km/h), an emergency escape often resulted in pilot injuries because the seat offered no protection for the pilot's face or extremities.

This first-generation Soviet ejection seat was used on the MiG-15, MiG-15bis, MiG-17, and La-15. Pilots were going to

need it, flying MiG-15 and MiG-15bis combat missions in Korea.

I-310—The MiG-15 Prototype

In 1946, the Mikoyan-Gurevich OKB was tasked by the Soviet government to develop a jet fighter capable of transonic speeds at high altitude, with an endurance of over one hour. This fighter would need the armament and avionics to enable it to cope with American and British warplanes of the era. The new fighter was also required to offer ease of maintenance.

Success depended on fulfilling requirements that seemed contradictory. A powerplant was decided upon with introduction of the Nene into series production in the USSR. Development of the ejection system in 1946–1947 also was

successful. As always, rigid convention came into conflict with pioneering concepts. Sometimes tradition prevailed but, in the main, scientific progress triumphed over orthodox solutions. Thus, the Mikoyan-Gurevich OKB chose swept wings on its fighter.

The Mikoyan-Gurevich OKB did not produce combat aircraft during the Great Patriotic War (the MiG-3 having been discarded by the end of 1941) and could spare time to design new fighters.

Mikoyan designers got acquainted with the swept-wing planform with the Utka (Duck) canard aircraft and with the moderately swept wing of the MiG-9 prototype. Development, testing, and production of the MiG-9 gave them experience with turbojet-powered fighters. But it was the straight-winged, rocket-powered I-270 ("G") interceptor that became

14

the first Soviet aircraft to achieve 621mph (1,000km/h), accomplished in 1947.

The MiG-15 did not become a production aircraft all at once. There were preliminary versions at several stages. After A. Mikoyan returned from England and Nene-1 engines were delivered, his OKB began development of the I-320 ("FN") tandem-engine night fighter. This was similar to the MiG-9 with side-by-side engines, except that the I-320's fuselage was adapted for tandem placement of the new engines. The I-320 had been in development from the beginning of 1947 and gave Mikoyan experience in designing tandem-engine jet aircraft. The initial decision to build a twin-engine version of the MiG-15 was dropped only when engine manufacturers could not provide a sufficient number of engines.

For the MiG-15, Mikoyan designers also considered a twin-boom version which looked like British Vampire. But a swept-wing version, later designated I-310, seemed simplest and most aerodynamically efficient.

To satisfy Voenno-Vozdushnye Sily (VVS; Soviet Air Force) requirements for takeoff and landing characteristics, and for a wing with a sweep angle of 35deg with 2deg anhedral, the idea of variable sweep arose in the Mikoyan design team.

This was in 1947, 30 years before the variable-sweep Mikoyan 23-11 (MiG-23 prototype) flew for the first time. Though the Mikoyan team familiarized itself with the German variable-sweep research, the time for a "swing wing" had not yet arrived, and in 1947 the designers selected another alternative.

It is necessary to point out that there were peculiarities in the Soviet aircraft industry. Super secrecy wrapped around the aircraft industry by the Komitet Gosudarstvennoy Bezopasnosti (KGB; State Security Committee) produced a situation where Soviet experts were well-informed about Lockheed and North American projects, but knew almost nothing about what other Soviet OKBs were doing. For this reason, designers often wasted time and money on duplicate efforts.

As for the I-310 development, the designers faced a problem that proved very hard to solve, namely providing the required c.g. location. With the engine in the rear fuselage, the c.g. was too far to the rear. This caused a degradation of stability and reduction of control effectiveness. The problem was solved in part by

The anti-spin rocket installed under the wing of the second prototype MiG-15 fighter. Test pilot Bogdanov was killed in this aircraft when he failed to recover from an inverted spin during testing.

extending the wing trailing edge.

A lot of problems were caused by the air inlet ducts. The shape of the ducts was strange because of the numerous obstructions they had to by-pass, including cockpit and fuel tanks. Outside air entered a subsonic intake divided by a splitter. Here, the air separated into two flows, directed along two ducts, by-passing the front avionics-equipment bay. Then these two air flows met at the engine inlet.

It was also necessary to prevent the rear fuselage from being overheated by exhaust gases while maximizing thrust. This problem was solved during flight tests of the first I-310 prototype. The fuselage was shortened and the size of the exhaust nozzle was reduced.

A separate challenge with the I-310 was how to accommodate its main landing gear in the wing because the I-310 lacked fuselage space for the undercarriage. Further, the wing was of three-spar, stressed-skin aluminium construction of high aspect ratio and might be weakened by the main gear bays. This prompted studies on how to develop a light yet rigid structure.

I-310 wing static strength tests were conducted at the Moscow Aviation Institute on a test bench. With the initial wing prototype, skin cracks appeared at 120 percent of maximum design load. Designers considered it possible to lighten the wing structure by 398lb (180kg). But then, the wing structure failed at only 70 percent of maximum load. Finally, as designers sought a balance between the strength they wanted and the weight penalty they did not want, the wing was reinforced and its weight increased by 40lb (18kg). Now, the wing structure failed exactly at the maximum design load. The designers were using what they called the "method of try-out and mistakes" because there existed no established way to predict strength characteristics in a swept-wing design. Lavochkin OKB engineer J.h Sverdlov created this technique while the La-160, La-168, and La-174 aircraft wings were being developed. His study, "Aircraft Structural Design," is considered a classic in Russia.

In July 1947, the MiG-9M (FR) made its first flight. This was the MiG-9 prototype. The future MiG-15 was going to need a pressurization system, and this MiG-9 prototype had a pressurized cockpit. The Yak-25 flew for the first time on 31 October 1947. This was the first aircraft in the USSR equipped with a ventilation-type, pressurized cockpit with air bleed from the engine compressor, designed by a Yakovlev team headed by G. Protasov. This system ensured normal pressure, temperature, and humidity con-

S-02 equipped with two external fuel tanks.

The 66gal (250ltr) external tanks were attached directly to the wing structure without pylons.

ditions in the cockpit and was perhaps closer to what the future MiG-15 would have.

Also with the Yak-25, a pneumatic canopy jettison system was developed, designed by L. Selyakov who later worked on the Myasischev M-4 and M-50 heavy bombers and, still later, was chief designer of the popular Tu-134 airliner. Just about all Soviet fighter canopies, including those on the La-15 and MiG-15, were based on Selyakov's work with the Yak-25.

Another problem facing designers of the I-310 was the positioning of its cannons. As decided first with the MiG-9, ar-

mament was a single N-37 37mm and two NS-23 23mm cannons. Initially, the I-310's cannons were to be mounted as on the MiG-9 (FL) testbed—with the 37mm cannon protruding from the inlet splitter and the 23mm cannons protruding far forward from right below the inlet—but during MiG-9 tests, pilot A. Kochetkov found that his engine often failed when his cannons were firing because the engines were ingesting the cannon-powder gases.

Kochetkov's test flights underscored the need for fast trouble-shooting. Following a review of possibilities, the cannons were mounted below the cockpit,

37mm on the right and two 23mm on the left. But there remained the question of how to remove and maintain them. The solution was simple and brilliant: the cannons were integrated into a single unit, installed as a package raised and lowered by hoist. Ammunition could be quickly replaced and the aircraft readied for its next flight.

The aircraft was equipped with OSP-48 simplified landing system for use under the IFR (instrument flight rules) conditions. This system used two radio beacons, three radio marker command sets, and HF or VHF radio direction finders to facilitate approach, descent to landing, and touchdown in bad weather. The fighter was also equipped with the ARK-5 automatic radio compass, RV-2 low-altitude radio altimeter, and MRP-48 marker receiver.

The first I-310 prototype, numbered S-01, was powered by a British Nene-1 turbojet delivering 4,928lb (2,230kg) thrust. Construction of S-01 began in the spring of 1947. By then, a mock-up had been reviewed by a VVS commission.

Flight-Testing

At the end of 1947, S-01 was completed and moved to the test airfield at Ramenskoye. V. Yuganov, who worked for Mikoyan from 1946 to 1949, was appointed test pilot for the prototype.

To keep to the planned schedule, S-01's maiden flight had to take place by the end of December. The weather was poor, and it was clear that it would be better to modify the plan rather than lose the only aircraft available. A decision was made to perform the first flight in the new year, 1948. But Yuganov was short of

A front view of the S-02. Note the stall fences on the upper surfaces of each wing. S-01 and S-02 were flown in State flight tests in 1948, after which the design was given the designation MiG-15.

The second I-310 fighter prototype.

money (the first flight was worth 10,000 roubles at that time in the USSR) and insisted that the first flight be performed before the end of 1947. On 30 December, the cloud-base height was 6,560ft (2,000m), which meant that the first flight could not be performed, according to the rules. Yuganov decided he would fly anyway, so he quietly climbed into the S-01 cockpit, the aircraft tractor carried the aircraft to the preliminary start position to save fuel, and he took off.

Yuganov retracted the landing gear, flew two circles below the cloud base, and landed. This first flight of the future MiG-15 took place without A. Mikoyan, head of the bureau. The chief designer congratulated Yuganov by phone.

Manufacturer's development tests began in 1948 and were completed in three months. Meanwhile, work proceeded on the second prototype, or S-02, which differed from S-01 in having a Nene-2 engine and a more complete avionics package. S-02 was also equipped with an ASP-1N optical gun sight and had increased aileron area.

In the USSR, an aircraft prototype often has a different avionics package from the production version. As a rule, some of the radio and navigational systems were not installed initially. If radar was envisaged, it was not installed at all, or a prototype was flown with an earlier, well-developed radar.

S-02 first flew on 27 May 1948. It was intended for official state flight tests at the Scientific and Research Institute of the Air Force (NII VVS).

In the summer of 1948, both prototypes were moved to the NII VVS test facilities at Chkalovskoye in the Moscow

suburbs. But even before state flight tests were completed, the decision was made to begin production.

State flight tests were performed in two stages, 27 May–25 August 1948, and 4 November–3 December 1948. During these tests, the I-310 received the designation under which it made its mark in history. It was now, officially, the MiG-15.

The third prototype, S-03, was built in March 1948, and was also earmarked for state flight tests. Like S-02, it was powered by a Nene-2. Hydraulic air brakes were installed in the rear fuselage, the empennage configuration was al-

tered, fuel capacity was increased, and provision was added to carry bombs under the wing. Its N-37D cannon was equipped with a flash suppressor. Test pilot I. Ivaschenko made S-03's first flight on 17 July 1948. Developmental tests were conducted through 15 October by Ivaschenko and S. Anokhin. Forty-five flights were made. The aircraft was found capable of a speed of Mach 0.934.

In November 1948, S-03 was transferred to the NII VVS airfield at Saki on the Crimean Peninsula, where it underwent further tests, completed on 23 December. At this point, Marshal K. Vershinin, commander-in-chief of the VVS,

The third prototype I-310 (S-03) during production tests. S-03 was first flown on 17 July 1948. It was powered by a Rolls-Royce Nene-2 turbojet engine. Among other changes, S-03 introduced hydraulic air brakes to the I-310 design. These air brakes were incorporated on the production MiG-15 and were increased in size on the later MiG-15bis.

Production tests of the S-03 were held from mid-July to mid-October 1948. The tests resulted in attaining a speed of Mach 0.934. Even before S-03 completed its final flight tests on 23 December 1948, the MiG-15 was ordered into production.

The La-15 fighter became the main competitor of the MiG-15 in the late 1940s. This photo depicts its second prototype, designated 174D, during development tests.

The Lavochkin OKB's jet fighter prototypes looked externally like the MiG-15, with swept wing, high-set stabilizer, and nose air intake. The La-15 differed in having fuselage-mounted landing gear structure and a high-mounted wing. The La-15 was also put into production, but it was soon discontinued because its wing design—made of many machined, rather than stamped parts, and with many complex joints—was too difficult and costly for sustained production.

signed an order to introduce the MiG-15 fighter into the VVS inventory.

Despite Vershinin's order, NII VVS pilots were still charged with determining which of two aircraft (MiG-15 or La-15) was preferable. The La-15 was faster and more stable at speeds approaching Mach 1, but military test pilots considered its main shortcoming to be its small wheelbase, which made the aircraft difficult to control during crosswind landings. The La-15 also rated poorly on ease of manufacture and maintainability. The process for manufacturing the La-15's wing, by machining major pieces from solid blocks of metal and mating them with complex joints, contributed to the downfall of the aircraft, since its production was very labor intensive.

It was decided to perform spin tests on these two aircraft. There was some experience with tests of this kind, similar experiments having been conducted for piston-engine aircraft. It was decided to increase the altitude at which a spin was entered, from 16,400ft (5,000m) to 22,960ft (7,000m), to be certain of safe recovery. An anti-spin rocket was installed under the wing of each aircraft. Though the tests were well-planned, NII VVS test pilots Y. Antipov and A. Kochetkov (the La-15 pilot) reported that both aircraft behaved strangely at high angles of attack.

The tests demonstrated that fighters' noses went up during spin entry. This meant the aircraft was about to stall into a flat spin, a peculiarity of the swept-wing configuration with high-set horizontal

tail. To add a further safety margin, the spin entry altitude was increased to 32,800ft (10,000m).

During an La-15 test flight, Kochetkov delayed spin recovery and had to use the anti-spin rockets. The MiG-15's spin behavior, according to test-pilot evaluations, was unconventional: during one turn, there took place two different spins, steep at first, than flat, each occurring alternately during a continuing turn.

At the initial stage of inverted spin tests, NII VVS test pilot Bogdanov could not recover and was killed in the second prototype. His colleague S. Brovtsev continued the MiG-15 spin tests. He specialized in swept-wing-fighter spin tests, flying the MiG-15 and La-15 in turn. Brovtsev investigated both conventional and inverted spin modes.

In one of the test flights, the aircraft refused to come out of an inverted spin. As altitude decreased, Brovtsev made repeated efforts to recover. He applied spin-provoking control inputs instead of typical anti-spin inputs. Finally, rotation halted only when altitude was down to a dangerous 1,968ft (600m). The test pilot leveled off and landed. Using test data to reconstruct pilot's behavior confirmed some of the MiG-15's peculiarities and helped to work out standard spin-recovery procedure for the MiG-15 flight manual.

After the NII VVS flight tests, both fighters were introduced into the VVS inventory. The La-15 soon was discarded because of its production complexity. The MiG-15, however, was destined for a long service life.

Chapter 2

The MiG-15, MiG-15bis, and UTI-MiG-15

A year after the first flight of the I-310 (S-01), the production MiG-15, MiG-15(s) flew for the first time (even Soviet sources give conflicting dates). Production of the Nene-2 jet engine, designated RD-45F, also began. In 1949, the first operational MiG-15 entered service with the VVS.

Production MiG-15s were not yet equipped with an automatic engine control system. There were no boosters (or hydraulic actuators) for the roll controls. The first aircraft cockpits were equipped with push button circuit breaker panel boards in the cockpit. This looked good but was very inconvenient to pilots, who called these buttons the "Russian accordion." Later, standard circuit breakers were employed instead, after which existing MiG-15s were found in two types, the "push-button" and "non-push-button" varieties.

The aircraft was not equipped with the OSP-48 IFR landing system at first, and time was required for it to become operational and for pilots to get used to it. As the MiG-15 matured, guns with a higher rate of fire were installed. There were other deficiencies to be eliminated as development proceeded: the aircraft maximum allowable speed corresponded to Mach 0.92, but initially (based on test flight results) it was restricted to Mach 0.88.

The reason for the limitation was the tendency of the wing to drop, or so-called wing stiffness asymmetry. On the production line, it was very difficult to make both wings absolutely identical, with the same stiffness (because of skin thickness variances, different rivet tightening, and so on). This structural and manufacturing asymmetry, in turn, caused the aerodynamic asymmetry. The wing on each side of the MiG-15 provided a different amount of lift. This difference was not noticeable at low speeds, but as the speed increased it became appreciable. At high speed the pilot was not able to offset the natural tendency of the aircraft to bank. Designers tried to eliminate this deficiency by toughening manufacturing discipline at aircraft plants and by adding trailing-edge control surfaces, called "knives" (bendable trim tabs), which were adjusted on each aircraft after an acceptance flight. Improved manufacturing largely solved the problem of wing symmetry, but the "knives" were retained.

The MiG-15 Enters Service

Introduction of the MiG-15 into inventory was a technical revolution in the VVS. The early Soviet jet fighters (Yak-15, Yak-17, and MiG-9) were not impressive, whereas the piston-engine Yak-3, Yak-9, La-7, La-9, La-11, and some Bell P-63 Kingcobras were still operational and were serving well. But when the first MiG-15s arrived, pilots and technicians knew they were encountering not just a new aircraft but a new era.

Initially the MiG-15s were operated only in daytime VFR (visual flight rules) conditions. Aerobatics, combat maneuvers, and spin entry were out of the question at first, but were employed as VVS units gradually placed the MiG-15 into service. Work on a fighter training version was begun and a large group of instructor pilots was created.

NII VVS test pilots visiting VVS units shared their experiences with the Soviet front-line pilots and trained them in IFR flight. Everybody, from sergeant technician to air regiment commander, received training. It was a time like 1941, when feverish pilot conversion training had taken place. Well-trained commanders were placed in charge of conversion training in MiG-15 combat units.

Some time later, VVS flight inspection groups were created in different regions of the USSR. Their main goal was to train pilots and monitor flying in different regions for uniformity of procedures and tactics. These groups were headed by very experienced military test pilots. For example, the Far East inspection group was headed by test pilot Maj. Gen. P. Stefanovsky, Hero of the Soviet Union, who had been first to master aerobatics in the first Soviet production jet fighter, the Yak-15.

The MiG-15 was brought into service in a remarkably short time. By mid-1950, some VVS units were combat ready. By 1952, all VVS tactical units flying the MiG-15 were deemed combat ready.

The MiG-15 was, in fact, an uncom-

Top to bottom: the first MiG-15 prototype was designated I-310 (S-01); a MiG-15bis with OSP-48 blind landing system and detachable external fuel tanks; a MiG-15bis of the Kubinka Air Division (nicknamed the "Parade" division as the Soviet Air Force's primary demonstration establishment); a Soviet MiG-15 in an early 1950s paint scheme that soon appeared in the Korean sky; a UTI-MiG-15 that was operated by the Voluntary Society for Support of the Soviet Army, Air Force, and Navy (DOSAAF) in 1970s; and a UTI-MiG-15P (ST-7) two-seat trainer equipped with the RP-1 Izumrud radar.

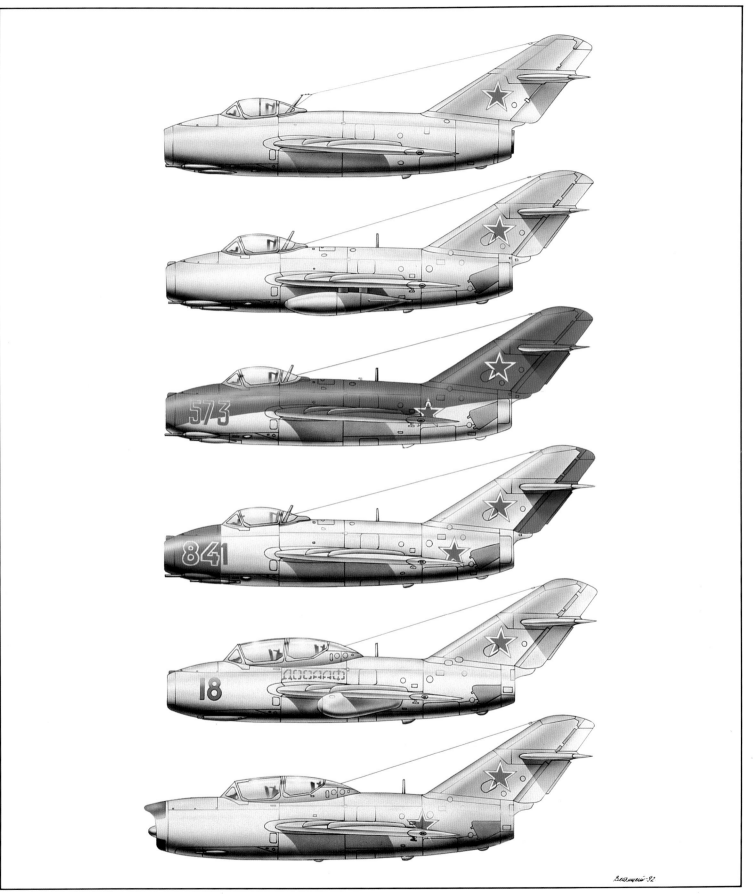

A prototype MiG-15 at the assembly shop of aircraft production plant No. 155 in Moscow.

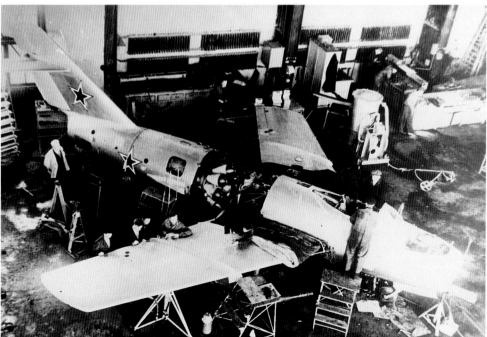

The MiG-15 on the assembly line. The removed fuselage skin reveals the engine, mounted in the center fuselage.

After the start of production and the completion of official State flight tests, air-brake panels were installed on the rear fuselage side surfaces as on this production MiG-15 (S).

The MiG-15 was tested by Scientific and Research Institute of the Air Force (NII VVS) and Flight Research Institute (LII) of the Aircraft Ministry test pilots. This MiG-15 is shown during evaluations at LII airfield Zhukovsky (Ramenskoye).

A MiG-15 on a test flight.

This aircraft, with call number 110 on its fuselage, is a production MiG-15 (S) taking off for a checkout test flight.

One of the MiG-15 prototypes while undergoing the production tests with a detached 37mm gun fairing.

The cockpit canopy of the MiG-15 opened by sliding to the rear and provide a front windscreen of bullet-proof glass.

The MiG's high-set stabilizer kept the rear control surfaces out of the wing's turbulent air.

The MiG-15's main landing gear strut folded toward the fuselage into the wing's lower surface.

Early production MiG-15 air-brake panels. Similar air brakes were installed on many MiG-15 modifications including the UTI-MiG-15 two-seater.

The upper surface of the wing had stall fences to improve wing aerodynamics.

The MiG-15 (S) escort fighter equipped with two high capacity 158gal (600ltr) external fuel tanks.

Production MiG-15s during military exercises in the late 1950s.

This photo shows the two-seat trainer version of the MiG-15, the UTI-MiG-15 Sparka, being towed to the runway during a training alert.

In late 1940s and early 1950s, an aerobatic team was organized at Kubinka Air Force base. Pilots of this team, predecessors of the current Russian Knights and Swifts, flew MiG-15s and participated in public displays at the Tushino air shows. Kubinka-based MiG-15s were painted in an original red and silver scheme. These aircraft flew many shows over Kubinka airfield demonstrating Soviet Air Force performance for top-ranking Soviet officials and representatives of Soviet-bloc countries. The best pilots at Kubinka flew MiG-15s as members of the aerobatic team.

monly simple and reliable aircraft. Its in-service nickname, "aircraft-soldier," meant that the MiG-15 was simple, reliable, unpretentious, and invulnerable. All of these qualities were to be needed in the first postwar conflict between the communist East and the free world in Korean skies.

While in production, the MiG-15 was repeatedly modified and updated. A major update in 1949 created the MiG-15bis version powered by the VK-1 engine. Other changes in MiG-15 equipment and armament were not always identified by new designations, among them the MiG-15bis airplanes with and without the OSP-48 landing system, and those with NS-23 and NR-23 cannons. Many MiG-15s were fitted with Bary-M IFF (identification, friend or foe) transponders, while others had no transponders.

The advent of new avionics required modification of the aircraft structure. Based on operational experience and combat use, especially combat operations in Korea, pilot armor was improved. Several versions of the UTI-MiG-15 Sparka trainers were built for advanced training. Baseline MiG-15s were used for photo reconnaissance and as escort fighters. At the last stage of its service life, the MiG-15bis served as a ground-attack aircraft with appropriate weapons alterations.

In addition, MiG-15bis and UTI-MiG-15s were built or converted in Czechoslovakia, Poland, and China. Although the total number of the MiG-15s manufactured cannot be stated with certainty, the probable figure is 7,000 to 7,500 in all countries.

Close formation takeoff of a group of MiG-15s during an air show.

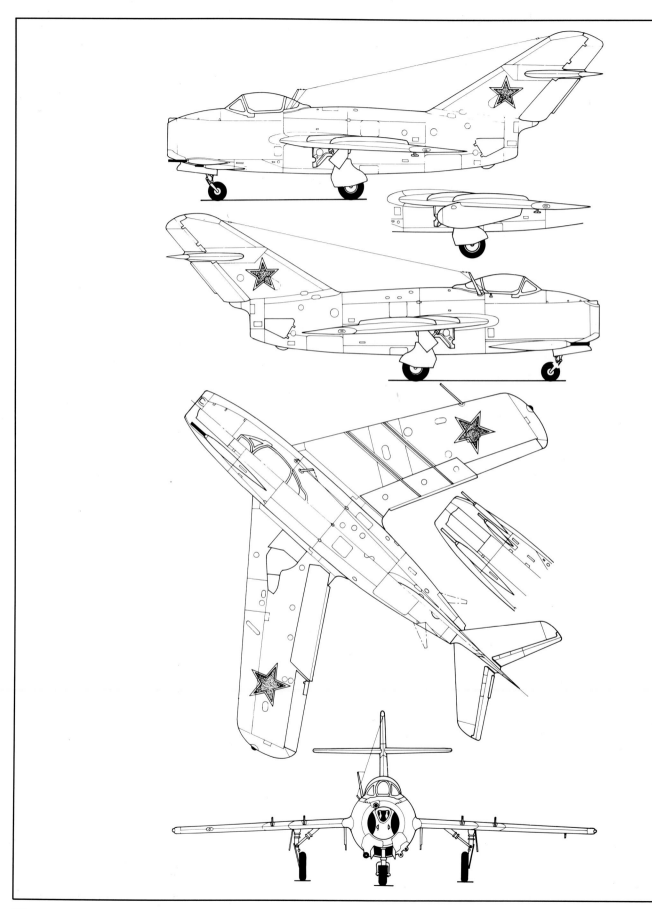

MiG-15 (SV)

The first production MiG-15 version, the MiG-15 (SV), was rolled out in June 1949. Improvements and new systems were introduced and later became standard in follow-on MiG-15 versions. Changes included:

• Two NR-23 cannons with a firing rate of 850 rounds per minute replaced two NS-23s (550 rounds per minute) with no increase in weight. A breechblock accelerator was introduced; a bilateral cartridge feeding mechanism simplified the mounting of the gun. The NR-23 could be mounted on both sides of the fuselage

• An ASP-3N automatic gun sight replaced the ASP-1 model

• The BU-7 hydraulic actuator was included in the aileron control system for the first time

• Elevator aerodynamic balance was increased 18–22 percent

• The slot between elevator and vertical stabilizer was decreased

• Brake flaps were actuated by a push-button control system

MiG-15 Aircraft Modifications (table)

Design Designation	Production Designation	Air Force Designation	Description
I-310	S-01		First prototype
I-310	S-02		Second prototype
I-310	S-03		Third prototype
	S	MiG-15	First production aircraft
	SV	MiG-15	Main MiG-15 batch
	SA-3	MiG-15	SV IFR with OSP-48 system
	SA-4	MiG-15	SV with many improvements
	SSh		Two SV-based prototypes with a new weapon system
	SO		Aircraft with enhanced armor
	SU		Prototype with a movable weapons system
I-312	ST-1	UTI-MiG-15	First fighter-trainer version
I-312	ST-2	UTI-MiG-15	Second pre-production trainer
	ST-7	UTI-MiG-15P	Interceptor with Izumrud-1 radar
	ST-8	UTI-MiG-15P	Interceptor with Izumrud-3 radar
	ST-10		Testbed for ejection system

Continued on next page

Previous page
A production MiG-15 (SV) with RV-2 radio altimeter, RSI-6 radio station, and NS-23 guns.

The first MiG-15 (SV) was completed in June 1949. The aircraft had a number of new systems.

MiG-15 Aircraft Modifications

Design Designation	Production Designation	Air Force Designation	Description
	SD	MiG-15bis	Modification with VK-1 engine
	SA-1	MiG-15bis	SD with OSP-48 IFR system
I-330	SI (Strela 45)	MiG-15bis	MiG-17 based on production MiG-15bis
	SD-ET		Improved production SD
	SD-UPB	MiG-15Sbis	Escort fighter
	SR	MiG-15Rbis	Reconnaissance aircraft
	SP-1	MiG-15Pbis	Interceptor with Tory radar
	SP-5	MiG-15Pbis	Interceptor with Izumrud-1 radar
	SL-5		Testbed with VK-5 engine
	SE		Testbed for wing and tail changes
	SD-5	MiG-15bis	SD fighter armed with rockets
	SD-57	MiG-15bis	SD fighter armed with rockets
	SD-21	MiG-15bis	SD fighter armed with rockets
	SD-25	MiG-15bis	SD fighter with PROSAB-250 bombs
	ISh	MiG-15bis	Fighter with reinforced wing and pylons
		MiG-15bis	With Garpun Burlaki system
		MiG-15bis with refueling probe	Fixed to receive a probe-and-drogue refueling system
	Czechoslovakia		
	S-102		Licence-produced MiG-15
	CS-102		Licence-produced UTI-MiG-15
	S-103		Licence-built MiG-15bis
	MiG-15Fbis		Photographic reconnaissance
	MiG-15T		Tow-target version of MiG-15
	MiG-15Tbis		Tow-target version of MiG-15
	MiG-15SB		Fighter-bomber version with enlarged armament package
	MiG-15SBbis		Fighter-bomber version with enlarged armament package
	UTI-MiG-15P		Interceptor with Izumrud-5 radar
	Poland		
	Lim-1		Licence-built MiG-15
	Lim-2		Licence-built Mig-15bis
	Lim-1.5		Conversion of Lim-1 to mount Lim-2 avionics
	SB Lim-1		Trainer version of Lim-1
	SB Lim-2		Trainer version of Lim-2
	SB Lim-1A		Spotter version of SB Lim-1
	SB Lim-2A		Spotter version of SB Lim-2
	SB Lim-2M		SB Lim-2A reconverted into a combat trainer
	China		
	J-2		MiG-15 operated in China and updated. Export designation F-2
	JJ-2		Licence-built UTI-MiG-15. Export designation FT-2

Notes: *MiG-15 prototype versions that did not have special designations and that differed from the baseline aircraft only in avionics and armament changes are not included in the list. Some flying testbeds used in the USSR and abroad about which there is no verifiable data, are not listed either.*

- The fuel feeding system was designed to provide stable pressure across a range of speeds and altitudes
- The engine starting panel was installed at frame 13 (earlier it was on the airfield trolley)
- A new cockpit control panel was introduced
- The DGMK-3 remote gyromagnetic compass replaced the earlier PDK-45 compass
- BANO-45 navigational lights replaced BO-39 models
- The 12-SAM-25 storage battery replaced 12-A-30

The SV aircraft went through two test phases, in June and October 1949. In the second phase all shortcomings were eliminated.

In the summer of 1950, tests were carried out with new pressurized landing gear strut shock absorbers. These were effective but did not enter production. Production aircraft had conventional main strut absorption and reduced-pressure nose-strut absorbers.

Because VVS units reported that the aircraft sometimes bounced uncontrollably on rough landings, the landing gear was tested until the problem was found. Famous Soviet test pilot S. Suprun conducted all types of test landings to isolate the problem. Suprun found that the aircraft forgave even a heavy three-point, high-flare landing but began to bounce during a high-speed landing. On his twenty-fifth landing, he was particularly rough, greatly exceeding all landing parameters from the flight manual, and the aircraft nearly turned over. Nose and starboard struts were severely damaged. His tests showed that the problem was caused by poor landing technique, rather than a problem with the aircraft. The absorber charging system and definitive landing gear could now be finalized.

The MiG-15 (SV) entered production and became the main single-seat, RD-45F-powered MiG-15 version.

The first production MiG-15 (SV)s were armed with NS-23 guns and a few with the OSP-48 system. In the final batch of SVs, the push-button circuit breakers were replaced by conventional circuit breakers. These late MiG-15 (SV) were assigned to units fighting in Korea and received their baptism of fire in that conflict.

In service, some MiG-15 (SV)s were retrofitted with improved avionics and

The MiG-15 (SV) had NR-23 guns instead of NS-23s and a new double-side cartridge supply system.

The MiG-15 (SV) during manufacturer's development tests. Readily visible are extended trailing edge flaps.

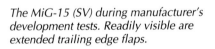

A production MiG-15 (SV) during checkout tests at the Scientific and Research Institute of the Air Force.

In the early 1950s, the MiG-15 (SV) became the main fighter aircraft of the Soviet Air Force.

other equipment. Some improved SVs were built in single sample only, and not further developed.

MiG-15 (SA-3)

In 1950, 15 production MiG-15s powered by RD-45Fs were converted for installation of the OSP-48 IFR landing system. The instrument panel arrangement was improved and the rear fuel tank was replaced with two tanks of less fuel capacity, making room for the ARK-15

compass and MRP-48 marker receiver units. The AFA-IM photographic camera was removed. The improved aircraft were transferred to the combat units, where OSP-48 IFR landing system familiarization and mastering began. Soon the OSP-48 became standard equipment for all MiG-15 versions.

MiG-15 (SA-4)

The MiG-15 (SA-4) was powered by the RD-45F and was equipped with the OSP-48. Compared to the basic MIG-15, it featured: improved instrument panel, generator failure warning indicator, KI-11 compass, a Mach meter that read up to to Mach 0.95 and provided automatic air-

brake extension if this speed was exceeded, DGMK-2 gyrocompass and the AGK-47B attitude indicator, an engine air starting system, and a landing gear control cock.

The MiG-15 (SA-4) completed developmental tests in August 1950 and was transferred to the NII VVS for flight tests. The innovations tested on the SA-4 were incorporated on production MiGs.

MiG-15 (SO)

Based on the VVS request, a single production MiG-15 (SV) with NR-23 guns was retrofitted with more armor for better pilot protection. The armored glass of its windshield was thickened and an ar-

This early production MiG-15 (SV) is exhibited in a town in Crimea.

This detachable gun mount was exhibited near a MiG-15 at the Soviet Air Force Museum in Monino.

The MiG-15 (SU) fighter was equipped with a flexible gun mount to allow the MiG's pilot to more easily lead his target and to fire at off-axis targets. The guns could be deflected upward 11deg and downward 7deg.

mored backrest and headrest added.

This aircraft was equipped with a sliding ASP-3N gun sight to decrease the number of pilot injuries during accidents, because it moved forward automatically in a crash so the pilot would not injure his head by striking it. It had two positions: stowed (retracted) and operational (extended).

This aircraft completed its flight test program in 1950. In early 1950 the MiG-15 (SO) high speed flight tests (Mach number exceeding 0.92) took place at the LII Flight Research Institute.

The main purpose of these tests was to get data on aircraft behavior at speeds higher than the maximum allowable. During these tests the aircraft reached Mach 0.92 in a dive, though the MiG-15 was not capable of this speed in level flight.

At altitudes of 41,000–44,280ft (12,500–13,500m) with the engine running at 12,000rpm, the pilot took the aircraft in level flight up to the peak speed, then went into a shallow dive with the engine reaching 12,300rpm. The pilot then accelerated up to the pre-planned Mach number. After this, he recovered from the dive with the engine at idling condition.

These high-speed (Mach 0.86) flights demonstrated that the intensity of the wing-drop problem was different for different MiG-15s. Thus, these flights required the pilot to know the peculiarities of each individual MiG-15.

MiG-15 (SU)

In 1949, Mikoyan began work on variable-angle armament for the MiG-15.

This aircraft was given the suffix SU but was based on the production MiG-15 (SV). A B-I-25-Sh-3 weapon system, developed by the B. Shpitalny OKB, was installed instead of standard armament. In accordance with an Aircraft Industry Ministry order of 14 September 1950, a production MiG-15 was converted for installation of this armament system, which included two 23mm Sh-3 guns in flexible mounts attached to the lower front of the fuselage, one on each side. The guns could deflect upward 11deg and downward 7deg.

The B-I-25-Sh-3 system included a sight post and remote electrical units that moved the gun. When a pilot had a target in his sights, he could push a tracking

The MiG-15 (SU)'s V-1-25-Sh-3 flexible gun mount system consisted of a faired-over mount on either side of the lower part of the air intake, each containing one 23mm Sh-3 cannon.

V-1-25-Sh-3 flexible gun mount with the barrels in the down position.

MiG-15 (SU) forward fuselage. Note V-1-25-Sh-3 flexible gun mount with the barrels in intermediate position.

The main instrument panel of the MiG-15.
Steve Zaloga

button, after which the guns would automatically track the target. Gun and sight movements were synchronized via an electromechanical selsyn transmission.

Work on the prototype was completed by 29 December 1950. Development tests began on 2 January 1951 and were accomplished on 27 March 1951.

On 20 June 1951, test pilot Y. Antipov ferried the prototype to the NII VVS airfield for official state tests, which began ten days later and ran to 10 August 1951. In all, 63 flights were performed. Some were tests of the original gun mounting. In the report on the official state flight tests, it was pointed out that variable-angle armament mounting improved the MiG-15s tactical performance. In 1953, Mikoyan continued development of movable gun armament. The MiG-17 (SN) prototype was equipped with the SV-25-MiG-17 weapon system, installed in its forward fuselage. This system included three 23mm TKB-495 guns.

The SN aircraft, like the SU, was tested, but not developed further. It was found not to be efficient at transonic speed.

MiG-15 (SSh)

In 1950, two production MiG-15s built at the Kuibyshev aircraft plant and powered by the RD-45F were converted with a single 23mm Sh-3 type and a single N-37 gun. The N-37 mounting was the same on the standard production MiG-15, but the left gun-mount panel was converted to the Sh-3 gun installation; the mounting points were altered for the Sh-3; new cartridge boxes were installed; gun-mount caps, hatches, and fuselage fairings were altered; and mounting collars were installed for the Sh-3 barrel.

The first aircraft underwent durability tests with the new Sh-3 guns from 13 July to 25 August 1950. The second aircraft was submitted for state flight tests on 1 July 1950 after preliminary check-out flying. Test results were unsatisfactory.

MiG-15bis (SD)

Creation of the 5,952lb (2,700kg)

A production MiG-15bis, manufacturer's number 105015, during tests at the Scientific and Research Institute of the Air Force in the summer of 1950. This aircraft carried a one-digit call number, rare for Soviet fighters.

thrust VK-1 engine resulted in radical updating of the MiG-15 to improve its performance.

Built in 1949 and assigned the in-house suffix SD, the new fighter integrated the results of a year's production and operational experience with early MiG-15s.

The SD prototype differed from the production MiG-15 as follows:

• The new VK-1 uprated engine of slightly larger dimensions was installed in place of the RD-45F

• Dimensions of the extension pipe were increased

• The interior contours of frames 21–28 were altered to permit installation of the new engine

• NR-23 cannons were mounted instead of NS-23s (though early batches retained the NS-23)

• The ASP-3N sight replaced the ASP-1N

• The structure of frames Nos. 3–5a was changed as a result of installation of the new cannons

• A tail cone of new design and dimensions was introduced

• To alleviate a tendency to pitch up when speed brakes were deployed, the design of the brakes was changed slightly

• A reversible hydraulic actuator, type BU-7, was installed in the fuselage as part of the aileron control chain (later production aircraft were fitted with a BU-1 hydraulic actuator in the wing)

• Elevator set-back balance was increased to 22 percent

• Aerodynamic balance of the elevator and rudder were improved by changing their leading-edge shape

• Aileron chord was increased by 21 percent of the wing chord to improve the aileron effectiveness

• A solenoid-operated valve, controlled by a button on the control stick, was introduced into the control channel to improve speed-brake control effectiveness

• The engine starting panel was moved from the engine starting trolley to aircraft frame 13

• A screen-type oil filter was introduced

• A GS-3000 generator was installed

• A DGMK-3 compass replaced the PDK-45 model

• A signal-flare panel was newly installed, with the color and number of flares used indicated

A production MiG-15, manufacturer's number 107019, which underwent tests at the Scientific and Research Institute of the Air Force in the summer of 1950.

The Soviet-built VK-1 turbojet, rated at 5,952lb (2,700kg) thrust, was a development of the British Rolls-Royce Nene-2 turbojets that the Soviets purchased from Britain in 1946. Equipped with this engine, the MiG-15bis became the best jet fighter in the world at the time it entered service.

The MiG-15's detachable gun mounts made reloading and servicing of the aircraft's cannons quick and easy. If necessary, fully loaded and serviced cannon mounts could be kept on the flight line to be loaded into returning aircraft for even quicker turnaround.

The MiG-15bis' enlarged air brake panel is shown in the extended position.

• Because of flight-test and operational problems with wing dropping, a "knife" trim tab 1.57in (40mm) wide, was riveted to the wing trailing edge; a similar knife 1.18in (30mm) wide was attached to the right aileron (later aircraft batches were equipped with special wing-fuselage joints that allowed the pilot to alter wing incidence in flight)

The manufacturer's flight tests of the SD began on 2 July 1949 and were successfully completed on 9 September 1949. Then, the prototype was transferred to the NII VVS for official tests. On their completion, the SD was recommended for series production. Soon, deliveries began of the aircraft originally designated the "MiG-15 with VK-1 engine." From 1951, this version was named the MiG-15bis.

Compared to the MiG-15, maximum speed of the MiG-15bis at low altitude was 16mph (26km/h) greater, rising from 651mph to 667mph (1,050km/h to 1,076km/h). Rate of climb from sea level increased from 138ft/sec to 151ft/sec (42m/sec to 46m/sec), service ceiling went up from 49,856ft to 50,840ft (15,200m to 15,500m), and range without external fuel tanks was extended from 992mi to 1,154mi (1,600km to 1,861km). Takeoff run was reduced by about 328ft (100m) and became 1,653ft (504m). Landing roll increased by 230ft (70m) and reached 2,886ft (880m), raising the question of whether a brake chute was necessary, and normal takeoff gross weight of the aircraft increased 526lb (238kg), reaching 11,147lb (5,044kg) be-

cause of the new engine, equipment, and armament.

Based on operational experience and lessons from testing of prototypes, the MiG-15 was repeatedly improved while in production. Between 20 May and 20 July 1951, work was carried out to shorten its landing roll. The UA-11 anti-skid control system was tested, as were three kinds of the drag chutes: the TP-1453-50, canopy area 78sq-ft (7.2sq-m); two TP-1453-50, total area 155sq-ft (14.4sq-m); TR-20, canopy area 220sq-ft (20.4sq-m). None of these chutes were judged to be satisfactory.

A fourth parachute, the PT-2165-51 of 162sq-ft (15sq-m) was also tested at the NII VVS from 4 to 20 September 1951. The braking system proved satisfactory and was recommended for series production. A developmental batch of MiG-15bis fitted with PT-2165-51 brake

chute and UA-11 antiskid control was produced by Kuibyshev aircraft plant No. 1 in 1952. These aircraft entered service.

Installation of NP-23 cannons in place of the NS-23 on the production MiG-15bis, which had been contemplated during development of the SD prototype, began in July 1951. The MiG-15bis was noticeably improved as a combat weapon system: the firing rate was increased more than 50 percent, the density of fire greater, and shell dispersion decreased.

Further, a program was carried out in 1951 to improve rearward vision. The canopy glass was 0.39in (10mm) thick. The rear canopy upright and canopy frame were removed (the framework was replaced with steel strips). The result was a new, transparent canopy that passed all tests in September 1951 and was recommended for production. Actual produc-

tion of the new canopy began in 1952.

Also during 1952, the MiG-15bis was equipped for the PPK-1 G-suit system. Air for the G-suit was bled from the engine compressor through an air intake pipe and was fed through a filter. Automatic pressure control governed the pressure differential in the chambers of the G-suit, based on the G-loads acting on the aircraft. The PPK-1 system operated within G-loads of 1.75–8, thus making it easier for the pilot to fly in combat at high G-loads.

During 1952, the speed brakes were increased in size with no change to the fuselage. Flight tests proved the new speed brakes more effective, improving dive characteristics at high altitude. That year, these speed brakes were placed into production.

The USSR's first rear-view periscopes were brought into practical use in the

MiG-15s were capable of carrying various external fuel tanks of 66–158gal (250–600ltr) capacity.

1950s. A contract was awarded by the Defense Ministry to the S. Vavilov Optical Institute to develop periscope types TS-23, TS-25, and TS-27; these were tested on the MiG-15bis two-pane canopy and MiG-17 single-piece canopy.

In June 1952, the TS-23 periscope was installed on one MiG-15bis for tests, a TS-25 on another. Tests showed both periscopes unsuitable for operational use: the TS-23 provided an inconvenient view with its inverted rear-view image, while the TS-25 lacked electrical defrost essential for combat at various altitudes and in different temperature conditions.

Based on test results, the Vavilov In-

МИГ-15 ТЕХНОЛОГИЧЕСКОЕ ЧЛЕНЕНИЕ

An exploded view showing the major assemblies of the MiG-15.

A production MiG-15bis during the check-out tests.

stitute developed the TS-27A periscope with a powerful electrical defrost system. This periscope was widely used on the MiG-17 fighter.

The MiG-15bis was the most numerous MiG-15 variant. It served with the VVS, Warsaw Pact countries, and Third World countries, and proved a reliable and effective weapon system. Like the MiG-15, the MiG-15bis was produced abroad. Some foreign-built aircraft had minor modifications.

Production MiG-15bis Technical Description

The MiG-15bis tactical fighter was intended for combat operation in VFR and IFR day and night weather conditions. A pressurized cockpit and an impressive service ceiling coupled with a high rate of climb made the aircraft capable of flying high-altitude, GCI (ground control intercept) missions.

The MiG-15bis was capable of carrying two external tanks of 106gal (400ltr) capacity under its wings using special pylons.

The MiG-15bis was built by several aircraft plants simultaneously in large quantities. It was called an "aircraft-soldier," reliable in combat and easy to maintain and operate.

The MiG-15bis underwent checkout tests at the Scientific and Research Institute of the Air Force more than once. This photo reveals a production aircraft with two external fuel tanks of 106gal (400ltr) capacity.

With powerful armament and a limited external bomb load, the MiG-15bis could be used as a fighter-bomber or attack aircraft. Its air-brake panels enabled the MiG-15bis to fly light dive-bombing missions. With 600ltr external fuel tanks, the MiG-15bis was able to fly escort missions. And the aircraft could be equipped with photographic equipment for recon missions.

The MiG-15bis was a mid-wing cantilever monoplane of all-metal structure with swept wing and empennage. Its landing gear was conventional, with the main-gear struts retracting into wing bays and the nose strut into the fuselage. The single Klimov VK-1 turbojet was mounted in the rear fuselage, behind the wing.

Fuselage

Fuselage length was 26ft 10.5in (8.08m), fuselage diameter 4ft 7in (1.45m), and the engine air intake diameter 2ft 5in (0.747m).

The fuselage was a semimonocoque structure formed of longerons, stringers, and a smooth, stressed skin integrating the fuselage framework into a single, rigid structure. The riveted fuselage structure was made mainly of D-16 duralumin. Type 30KhGSA steel was used for the joints. Attachment of the frames to longerons was made of steel.

Engine maintenance was eased via the engine removal fuselage break point frame 13, which divided the fuselage into front and rear sections. The forward fuselage ran from frame 1 to frame 13. It contained two elliptical air ducts spread along the fuselage boards and rounding the cockpit from the left and right sides. Equipment, including battery, oxygen bottles, RSIU-3 radio station, and Bary-M IFF responder, was installed in the compartment between frames 1 and 4. The nose landing gear bay was in the lower section of the forward fuselage. The armament bay and one more equipment compartment including RV-2 radio altimeter, MA-250 transformer, and ARK-5 radio compass receiver, were arranged below the cockpit. The fuel tank was installed between the frames 9 and 13.

Wing front and rear attachments were installed at frames 9 and 13. Frame 13 carried the engine mount with ten attachments. Frame 1 had a flanged cutout for the S-13 gun camera. The nose fairing with air intake splitter was attached to this frame.

There were four forward spars (two upper and two lower) in the fuselage section from frame 1 to frame 9 and four back spars from frame 9 to frame 13. Besides this, the auxiliary central upper spar was arranged between frames 11 and 13. The spars were attached to each frame by welded gusset plate made of steel.

The rear fuselage ran from frame 14 to frame 28 and contained the VK-1 (VK-1A) turbojet with its accessories and jet pipe, two-section rear fuel tank, control surface rods, air-brake flaps, signal rocket discharger, and PTsR-1 fuel pump.

The MRP-48 marker receiver, PRP-48 antenna, and ARK-5 antenna were served by a detachable cover on the lower hatch. Structurally, the lower fin was integrated with the rear fuselage.

The structure of the rear fuselage consisted of transverse framework including 15 frames and longitudinal framework including ten spars and a number of stringers, supporting the skin.

Air-brake panels of 5.2sq-ft (0.48sq-m) total area and 55deg deflection angle were mounted between frames 26 and 28 on both sides of the fuselage. The engine jet pipe was attached to frame 28, the final frame, via a special attachment point.

Cockpit

The pressurized cockpit was arranged in the center of the fuselage, be-

44

Two external fuel tanks of 106gal (400ltr) capacity gave the Mig-15bis the range for bomber-escort missions.

ween frames 4 and 9. The cockpit canopy consisted of two main parts: windscreen and the movable canopy. The rearward sliding canopy had a flat, armored windscreen almost 3in (64mm) thick. The duralumin windscreen frame was hermetically riveted to the forward fuselage structure. The movable canopy slid backward on guide rails and could be jettisoned in an emergency.

The cockpit was equipped with an ejection seat with guide rails at the back, and control panels with navigation, engine control, and other instruments, some on the floor and some on side consoles.

Pressurization made it possible to fly without oxygen up to 29,520ft (9,000m). The cockpit ventilation system cooled the cockpit at low altitude in hot weather.

Wing

The MiG-15bis had a sweptback wing consisting of two detachable outer wing panels with a joint at the fuselage. Each outer wing was equipped with a flap, sliding rearward during deflection, and an aileron with internal aerodynamic compensation.

The all-metal, stressed-skin wing structure comprised a longitudinal framework (forward spar, main spar, auxiliary rear spar, and a set of stringers) and a transverse framework consisting of two beams. Walls of the transverse and longitudinal beams together with the main beam formed the main gear wells.

Each outer wing panel had a detachable wing tip attached to rib 20 via

The MiG-15bis, powered with the Klimov VK-1 turbojet rated at 5,952lb (2,700kg) thrust instead of the RD-45 delivering 5,005lb (2,270kg) of thrust, offered improved speed and range.

The MiG-15's external fuel tanks were equipped with triangular tail surfaces to improve aerodynamics during aircraft-tank separation.

screws and anchor nuts. Each outer wing panel carried an anti-flutter weight.

The landing lights retracted into the space between the forward spar, rib 1, and the longitudinal beam of the left outer wing panel. The main-gear wells were covered by hinged doors, one installed on the forward spar and another on the main gear strut. The wing-fuselage joint was covered by a wing-root fillet attached to fuselage and wing by screws and anchor nuts.

The upper surfaces of the outer wing panels had stall fences aligned with the axis of aircraft.

A ground-adjustable trim tab was riveted to the trailing edge of each outer wing panel. A pitot tube was installed on the starboard outer wing panel between ribs 15 and 16.

Wing area was 221.9sq-ft (20.6sq-m), and wingspan 32ft 8.5in (10.18m). At quarter-chord, sweep angle was 35deg, the leading edge sweep angle being 37deg, and 2deg anhedral. Aspect ratio was 4.85, taper ratio 1.61.

The single-spar ailerons with 12 ribs and duralumin skin of 0.0314in (0.8mm)

thick were actuated via a reversible booster and were internally balanced. The port aileron had a trim tab.

The aircraft had hydraulically actuated, single-spar, TsAGI-type flaps (derived from Fowler-type flaps). The flaps had tip a stringer, auxiliary stringers, 19 ribs, and a duralumin skin.

Empennage

The MiG-15bis had a cantilever, sweptback empennage. The tailplane had a sweep angle of 40deg in plan. Tailplane and fin had a symmetrical profile of NACA-0009 type.

The tailplane consisted of a vertical fin with rudder and a horizontal stabilizer with elevators. The fin consisted of two parts: upper and lower. The upper part was connected to the lower by screws and was easily detachable. It was necessary to detach the upper fin in order to remove the horizontal stabilizer. The rudder also consisted of upper and lower parts, connected by cardan joint.

Control System

The MiG-15bis had conventional flight controls: elevators, ailerons, rudder, elevator trim tab control, aileron trim tab, flaps, and air brakes.

The control stick was connected with elevators and ailerons by push-pull rods, control cranks, and levers. The reversible

BU1 hydraulic actuator at the front spar of the starboard wing, as part of the aileron control system, reduced force on the stick.

Rudder control was performed by the pedals, rigidly linked to the rudder by push-pull rods, cranks, and levers.

Elevator trim tabs and ailerons were remotely controlled via UT-6D electric motors, transmitting movement to them through a system of levers and rods.

Flap control was actuated by hydraulic cylinders, installed in the wings. The flap control mechanism of the port and starboard flaps were linked by ropes to provide synchronous operation. The flaps moved rearward and simultaneously were deflected downward upon operation of the hydraulic cylinders. The flaps had two deflected positions: for takeoff and landing.

Air brake panels were controlled by pressing a button at the upper-left side of the control stick or by a tumbler on the left instrument panel. Synchronous deployment of the brake flaps was assured by their mutual mechanic link via levers, connecting rods, and a rigid torsion tube.

Undercarriage

To aid in safe landing, the MiG-15bis had tricycle landing gear, flaps, and air-brake panels. Some aircraft manufactured in 1952 were equipped with a brake chute.

The landing gear consisted of two main struts and a nose strut. Main-gear struts were attached to the wing structure and retracted into the wing roots. The nose-gear strut was attached to the forward fuselage and completely retracted forward into the fuselage, against the direction of flight. In retracted position the landing gear struts were fixed by locks. In extended position they were secured only by hydraulic locks. Landing gear wells were covered by doors when the wheels were up.

The position of undercarriage was indicated by warning lamps on the control panel and by mechanical indicators on the landing gear struts. All three landing gear struts had oil/pneumatic shock absorbers. The main-gear struts had 600x160mm wheels with single-side drum brakes. The nose gear was a 480x200mm wheel with a castor and shimmy damper.

Hydraulic system

The MiG-15bis' hydraulic system

was intended to actuate landing gear, flaps, air brakes, and the hydraulic booster, using an alcohol and glycerine mixture. The hydraulic system included the tank, low-pressure reduction gear, a pump installed at the gear box of the engine, a hydraulic accumulator, filter, protecting and return valves, manometer, a network of tubes, and accessories.

Pneumatic system

The aircraft pneumatics consisted of primary and emergency systems. The primary pneumatic system was intended for control of the main wheel brakes, cockpit pressurization, and recharging of armament. The emergency system was intended for landing gear and flap emergency extension and for emergency braking. The pneumatic system consisted of valves, reduction gearboxes, high pressure air bottles, cocks, pipelines, and flexible hoses.

Powerplant

The MiG-15bis was powered by a single Klimov VK-1 (VK-1A) turbojet with centrifugal compressor, single-stage turbine, and nine circular combustion chambers, delivering maximum static thrust of 5,922lb (2,700kg).

The powerplant included a gear box with oil pump box, accessories for fuel and electrical equipment, a single-stage centrifugal compressor with double-side air intakes, nine straight-flow combustion chambers, a single-stage axial turbine with nozzle box, and a jet tube with a conical nozzle.

The engine was mounted via four attachment points: two trunnions on the right and left sides of the compressor casing below the axis of the engine and two mounting lugs, arranged in the upper part of the engine. The engine was positioned behind frame 13. When the rear fuselage was detached, the engine remained sus-

The MiG-15bis was used widely in Aviation of the Soviet Navy. Shown is a group of naval pilots during a preflight briefing.

pended, protruding back from the forward fuselage.

Fuel system

Fuel system of the MiG-15bis consisted of two tanks of 372.5gal (1,410ltr) total capacity. The main flexible tank, contained in the forward fuselage between frames 9 and 13, held 330.2gal (1,250ltr) of fuel. A metal tank of 42.3gal (160ltr) capacity was arranged in the rear fuselage between frames 21 and 25 and consisted of left and right sections, each of 21.2gal (80ltr) capacity.

The aircraft used T-1 fuel, equivalent to JP-4 in the West. Fuel consumption was measured by a fuel gauge mounted

The MiG-15bis also served with the Voluntary Society for Support of the Soviet Army, Air Force and Navy (DOSAAF) to train young jet pilots.

on the main tank. A reserve of 79.3gal (300ltr) was indicated by a red signal lamp in the cockpit. Fuel was pumped from the rear tank by a PTsR-1 electric pump. The pump was situated in the lower engine section between frames 20 and 21. The SD-3 sensor monitoring operation of the pump was installed near it.

The fuel was burned as follows: 91.1gal (345ltr) was used from the main tank, followed by all fuel from the rear tank, followed by the remainder from the main tank. This was necessary to maintain the center of gravity of the aircraft.

Fuel was delivered by rubber hose to the PNV-2 pump from the main tank, mounted at the lower plate of this tank, and then to a shut-off cock behind frame

13. From the shut-off cock, fuel was delivered to the low-pressure filter and then to the engine. The system provided for defueling via a drain cock installed in front of the low-pressure filter. Fuel could be jettisoned using the same cock. All fuel tanks were equipped with a vent system.

The MiG-15bis was capable of carrying external fuel tanks of 66, 79.3, 105.7, and 158.5gal (250, 300, 400 and 600ltr) capacity to improve range. Tanks were mounted on standard carriers of BD2-48, BD3-53, and D4-500 type. External fuel tanks were pressurized by the engine compressor, and fuel was fed from them to the main tank under pressure.

With external fuel tanks installed, the order of fuel use changed: 26.4gal (100ltr) from the main tank, followed by all external fuel, followed by 66gal (250ltr) from the main tank, followed by fuel from the rear tank and, finally, the remainder from the main tank. A lamp in the cockpit signaled the use of external fuel.

Electrical System

The MiG-15bis' electrical system relied on a single-wire scheme of 28.5v. The total length of electrical wires in the aircraft was 24 mi (38km). Electrical system controls were arranged at the right and the left instrument panels of the cockpit.

Navigational Equipment

Navigational equipment was arranged on the main instrument panel and on the side consoles of the cockpit. It consisted of KUS-1200 airspeed indicator, VD-17 altimeter, RV-2 radio altimeter, AGI-1 gyro horizon, EUP-46 turn indicator, VAR-75 rate-of-climb indicator, DGMK-3 gyro-magnetic compass indicator (the compass itself was installed at the starboard outer wing panel), M-0.95 Mach meter, and ARK-5 radio compass indicator.

Radio Equipment

Radio equipment consisted of a simplified OSP-48 IFR landing system includ-

ing ARK-5 automatic radio compass with loop omnidirectional aerial, RV-2 radio altimeter with two aerials on the left outer wing panel and in the lower forward fuselage, MRP-48 marker receiver, Bary-M IFF transponder with an antenna installed in the upper part of the rear fuselage, and RSIU-3 VHF radio with whip aerial installed at the right side of the cockpit.

Survival Aids

The MiG-15bis was equipped with an ejection seat with ribbon-type parachute. Ejection was accomplished by pressing the canopy jettison handle, located on the seat.

Armament

The MiG-15bis was armed with one 37mm N-37 gun (starboard) weighing 227lb (103kg) with 40 rounds and two 23mm NR-23 guns (both on the port side of the fuselage) each weighing 86lb (39kg) each with 80 rounds. The larger cannon fired 400 rounds per minute, the

two smaller cannons 800-950 rounds per minute. The guns were recharged by a compressed air system. Recharging buttons were arranged on a special panel to the left of the sight. Gunfire was controlled electrically by pressing the button for the appropriate gun. The firing button for the N-37 gun was on the upper part of the stick and was protected by a guard. The firing button for both NR-23 guns was in upper forward part of the stick. The guns could be salvoed by pressing both buttons. The larger cannon could fire up to 6sec uninterrupted, the smaller cannons for 5.3sec. Links and ejected cartridge cases were discarded during firing. The aircraft was equipped with an ASP-3N automatic gun sight. An S-13 gun camera, mounted in the forward fuselage, was intended to record the results of firing and bombing. The electrical gun camera control made it possible to fire the cannons while photographing the result.

The MiG-15bis was capable of carrying two 110lb (50kg) or 220lb (100kg)

In the early 1970s, this MiG-15bis was exhibited at the Soviet Army Museum in Moscow, but it has since been moved.

bombs. Bomb release was actuated electrically.

MiG-15bis (SA-1)

The early MiG-15bis lacked a complete avionics and equipment package to efficiently exploit its tactical capabilities. The aircraft required the OSP-48 IFR landing system, and the system was retrofitted using modifications developed on the MiG-15 (SA-3).

In addition, the RSIU-3 VHF radio replaced the RSI-6 HF radio, a Bary-L IFF transponder was installed, a BU-1 hydraulic actuator was mounted in the wing leading edge, a new cooling and heating system was introduced, and the canopy had single-piece glass transparencies.

In order to keep weight within permissible limits the aircraft was stripped of

49

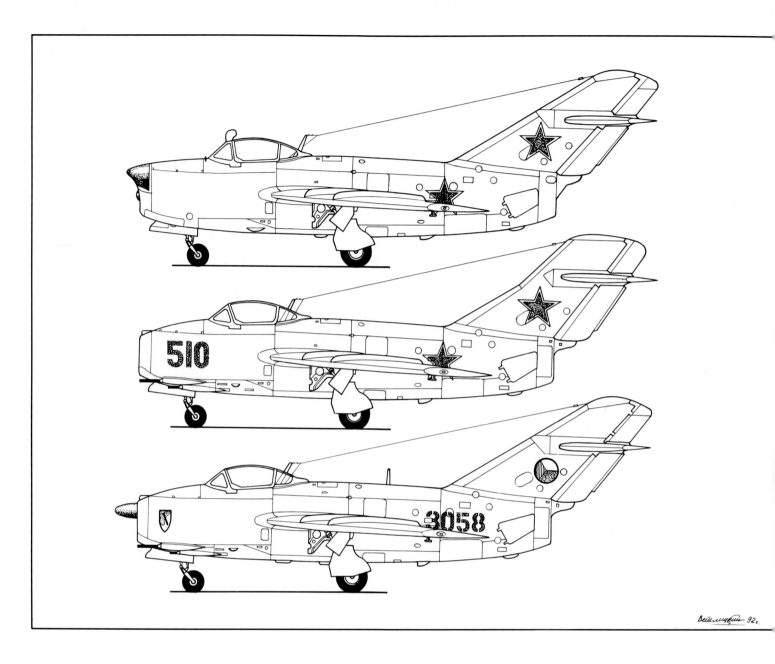

Top to bottom: a MiG-15bis (SP-5) prototype. This aircraft was used for the development of the RP-1 Izumrud radar which later was widely used by Soviet interceptor-fighters; and a MiG-15bis (SE) test bed; Czech modernization of the MiG-15bis, Mig-15SBbis fighter-bomber with PPZ-1 landing system.

the AFA-IM aerial camera, SOPT pressure differential warning indicator, VS-46 altitude switch, gun rounds counter, and armor plate on frame 5a.

The MiG-15bis (SA-1) underwent developmental flight tests in February and March 1950, followed by official tests.

Based on the the latter, the OSP-48 system was recommended for production.

MiG-15bis (SD-UPB) and MiG-15Sbis

The advent in the late 1940s of the first Soviet jet tactical bombers, the Il-28 and Tu-14, created a need for an escort fighter capable of 560mph (900km/h), with a range of at least 1,550mi (2,500km). The prop-driven La-11 escort fighter had the range but was not fast enough.

A decision was made, and a program initiated in 1950 to design an escort fighter based on the MiG-15bis, with large-capacity external fuel tanks.

A MiG-15 produced by plant No. 21 was equipped with jettisonable external fuel tanks with a capacity of 309gal (1,170ltr). New tank shackles of the D4-48 type were mounted, and this necessitated changing the wing shackle support pylon to employ BD2-48MIG pylons. Oxygen quantity was increased from 1.6gal to 2.1gal (6ltr to 8ltr). This aircraft and subsequent MiG-15s were fitted with expander-tube brake wheels.

The external fuel tanks were all-metal, of welded construction. The aircraft was tested from 10 June to 21 July 1950. Afterward, it underwent official tests and was returned for developmental work.

From 5 to 19 September 1950 the MiG-15bis was further tested with three external tank configurations: with a production tank of enlarged size; with the tank axis displaced 2in (50mm) toward the fuselage center line; and with a wooden mock-up with a thinned top and blended shape. According to test results, the wooden mock-up best met requirements. Metal test models of 158gal (600ltr) capacity were constructed and forwarded for official tests. In November 1950, the escort-fighter version of the MiG-15bis, designated MiG-15Sbis (SD-UPB), underwent development tests with the tanks. In January 1951, the SD-UPB was sent to the NII VVS for repeated check tests and passed them satisfactorily. According to the test report, the 158gal (600ltr) external tanks allowed the MiG-15bis to operate up to speeds of Mach 0.85. With the changes, the aircraft was put into production and given the designation MiG-15Sbis.

The production MiG-15Sbis fitted with 600ltr fuel tanks had a maximum range of 1,565mi (2,520km) at an altitude of 39,360ft (12,000m). Maximum flight endurance was 3hr, 52min. By comparison, the MiG-15bis without external tanks had a range of only 826mi (1,330km) and endurance of 2hr, 6min at the same altitude. Fuel capacity of the MiG-15Sbis was 689gal (2,612ltr). Take-off weight reached 13,494lb (6,106kg).

It should be noted that many external fuel tanks were developed for the MiG-15 and MiG-17 in the mid-1950s.

MiG-15Rbis (SR)

Early MiG-15s carried the AFA-IM aerial camera. The camera was unsatisfactory, so in 1950 it was removed to make space for new equipment. Now plans evolved to create a dedicated "recce" version of the MiG-15bis.

The prototype, assigned the company designation SR, was built by equipping a production OSP-48–equipped MiG-15bis with an AFA-BA/40 aerial camera with a focal distance of 40mm, for photo mapping. The camera was controlled from a command panel in the cockpit. The camera replaced one of the 23mm cannons. The S-13 gun camera remained. The SR aircraft passed development and official flight tests followed by a program aimed at improving its pressurized cockpit. The upgraded cockpit was recommended for production.

The MiG-15Rbis (SR) reconnaissance aircraft undergoing manufacturer's development tests.

During 1951, development of the aerial camera continued on the recce prototype. After rig tests and mounting of the camera, the SR (also called the SR-1) was sent for repeated proof tests to the NII VVS. The tests ended on 10 July 1951. The camera was approved and recommended for production.

The SR was series-produced as the MiG-15Rbis and usually flew with external fuel tanks. The MiG-15Rbis was in service for a long period until replaced by recce aircraft based on more modern combat planes.

MiG-15bis (SD-ET)

During 1950, the MiG-15bis underwent the following improvements, some of which were introduced into production:

• An ART-8 acceleration control unit was installed since the new VK-1 engine was prone to abrupt movement of the throttle control level at high altitudes

• A PN-2FAK fuel-flow restrictor was

51

Two 158gal (600ltr) external tanks installed under the wing of the MiG-15Rbis (SR) fighter-reconnaissance aircraft extended the flight range of the fighter significantly.

added to eliminate engine overspeeding
- A DK-6K minimum-fuel-pressure limiter was fitted to provide steady operation of the engine at low rpm
- Independent engine starting with a ST2-48 starter was introduced
- A GF-1103 chemical filter was installed into the air-conditioning system to clean air supplied to the cockpit
- The NR-23 cannon back-plates were strengthened
- Wing stiffness was increased to prevent wing dropping at high Mach numbers
- Pressures in the nose-landing-gear strut and in the tires were reduced to prevent damage to the tail during hard landings
- Pressure in the hydraulic system was decreased to improve system operation
- A Mach meter was mounted that automatically initiated speed brake deployment at a preset speed
- The external tank jettisoning pattern was changed, enabling the pilot to jettison tanks individually

The aircraft, assigned the company designation SD-ET, underwent development tests followed by official tests. These succeeded, and the green light was given to the MiG-15bis (SD-ET).

MiG-15bis (SP-1)

In the 1950s, NATO air forces began flying jet bombers capable of nuclear strikes on the USSR from European and Asian bases. The speed of these jet bombers made interception by visual means almost impossible in all but the clearest weather, so Russia's new task was to equip its interceptors with airborne radars.

On December 7, the chairman of the Council of Ministers issued a decree dictating creation of an airborne radar for interceptors.

Considering the complexity involved, the scientific research institutes and OKBs with the most expertise were entrusted with development of the radar. Three aircraft OKBs joined in the program.

The Mikoyan team chose a radar developed by A. Slepushkin's OKB. Named the Tory, this was of single-antenna type and operated in the cm-wave band. From the outset, designers intended this radar for the MiG-15 fighter.

As designers saw it, the Tory was favored because, having just one antenna, it did not greatly change the MiG-15's shape. Automatic target tracking devices were not yet reliable, so tracking had to be performed by the pilot, or by a radar operator if a two-seat version was developed. Mikoyan designers explored both concepts—a single-seat SP-1 (based on the MiG-15bis) and a two-seat, twin-engine heavy interceptor, the I-321(R), both with Tory-M radar.

The MiG-15bis (SP-1) was based on the production MiG-15bis. Radar and antenna were mounted in the forward fuselage. The antenna was located on top of the air intake, only slightly reducing the intake cross section. The aircraft became 4.7in (120mm) longer because of the radar antenna. The shape of the tail where it joined the fuselage also had to

be altered slightly since the diameter of the extension pipe of the VK-1 engine was increased.

Armament was reduced to a single 37mm N-37D cannon on the starboard side, with 45 rounds. The S-13 gun camera was mounted on the right. Wing and tail surfaces were similar to those of the production MiG-15bis, except for a larger wing setting angle and increased elevator and rudder aerodynamic balance.

The SP-1 was completed during 1949 and was test-flown by A. Chernoburov and G. Sedov from 23 April 1949 to 20 January 1950. This was followed by official tests from early January to 20 May 1950. Testing showed that wing dropping affected the SP-1 as well. Inboard fences on both wings were strengthened, thus increasing wing torsional stiffness and easing the problem.

From 23 to 29 August 1950, the SP-1 was subjected to further developmental tests. It was then decided to build a small batch of these aircraft. During 1951, five MiG-15bis were converted to Tory-M radar-equipped SP-1 standard. One of the five SP-1s was sent on 25 November 1951 to the NII VVS for proof tests. Military test and service pilots flew the aircraft and made intercepts. Il-28 and Tu-4 bombers were intercepted successfully.

The radar installed on the SP-1 was practical only for the most experienced pilots because they were required to fly the aircraft to the intercept and track the target simultaneously. For the average pilot this was too difficult, so Mikoyan switched to a two-antenna Izumrud radar system developed by V. Tikhomirov, leaving work on a single-antenna system for a future time when reliable automatic target tracking equipment could be designed.

Slepushkin continued development of his radar: a Tory-A prototype was built, then, based upon it, a new Korshun airborne radar. Both were flight-tested on the I-320 and SP-2, the latter being a follow-on to the SP-1 with the same engine, but with a 45deg swept wing. Neither system was put into production or went into service because the radars did not work.

After Stalin's death and normalization in the country, advanced technologies began developing rapidly, and permitted the USSR to compete with the West. This led to quick design and development of interceptor and attack radars

MiG-15bis (SP-1) prototype equipped with Tory-type radar.

The Tory radar aerial was mounted in the upper air intake section and covered by large fairing. The MiG-15bis (SP-1) prototype equipped with Tory radar had armament consisting of a right side N-37D gun only.

using reliable electronics, which permitted operational radars on Soviet interceptors by the late 1950s.

MiG-15bis (SP-5)

In the early fifties Mikoyan was involved in development of radar-equipped interceptors. Two types of radars were under development in the USSR at that time: autonomous radars and radar sights integrated with ordinary optical sights.

The OKB led by V. Tikhomirov started designing the RP-1 Izumrud radar sight in 1948. This project was considered to be of minor importance, mainly as back-up against possible failure of the Tory autonomous radar. The Izumrud provided search and automatic tracking of the target and determination of firing data with the ASP-3N optical sight, and it was linked to the IFF system.

In three years of hard work, the Izumrud radar was designed. It had two aerials—one for search mode, another for aiming and tracking. In search mode the radar was capable of looking through plus 60deg in bearing and plus 26 to minus 14deg in elevation in 1.33sec. It could acquire targets at up to 7.5mi (12km). The Izumrud operated in the centimeter-wave band. The transmitter power was 50–60 kW. The cathode-ray tube with high storage (may be retention or viewing) time allowed observing a great number of targets simultaneously.

Interception was performed in the following way. The interceptor switched on the radar sight and looked through the target zone in tracking mode. The ASP-3N display indicated the target as a tick, with the wingspan depending on the target's range. Tracking mode was switched on after the target was in a 7deg forward cone and within about 1.2mi (2km). The ASP-3N's computer determined the data for firing and gave the command to start the fire. The sight display indicated artificial horizon marks to simplify piloting while targeting. The sight was accurate to 1deg and 492ft (150m) at this range.

Mikoyan decided to use the RP-1 Izumrud radar sight on its interceptor. The major problem in fitting the RP-1 was in deciding how the two aerials should be arranged in the nose fuselage of the aircraft. It was decided to place the

search sight atop the air intake lip and the tracking sight aerial at the air intake inlet (splitter). This arrangement became standard for all Mikoyan aircraft carrying the Izumrud radar.

To implement this upgrade, the production MiG-15bis with VK-1 engine was converted to receive the Izumrud radar. The forward fuselage altered somewhat. The aerials for the RP-1 were enclosed in radomes. Provision was made for the Bary-M IFF transponder. Armament was reduced to two NR-23 cannons with 120 and 90 rounds for left and right, respectively. The S-13 gun camera was relocated to the forward fuselage starboard side. The second S-13 gun camera was arranged atop the canopy windscreen to photograph through the sight reticle. The aircraft was fitted with simplified OSP-48 landing system and HF ratio, type RSI-6.

The interceptor prototype with the bureau's designation SP-5 was built in 1950. It was tested in-house from 22 August to 9 September 1950. An Izumrud radar test and development program followed, lasting until 30 July 1951. On completing radar development, the SP-5 was submitted to NII VVS for evaluation which proved successful.

The Izumrud radar went into service in 1952 in MiG-17P and MiG-17PE fight-

The MiG-15bis (SP-5) prototype fighter equipped with RP-1 Izumrud radar. The RP-1 radar was developed into the RP-2, RP-3, and RP-5 radar sights used on later MiGs.

ers. Subsequently, the RP-1 radar was used as a basis to develop the RP-2, RP-3, and RP-5 radar sights, used on MiG-17PFU and MiG-19PM interceptor-fighters armed with SARH (semi-active radar homing) missiles of the type RS-2US(K-5).

MiG-15bis (SL-5)

During June and July 1951, Mikoyan retrofitted production MiG-15bis aircraft with the new VK-5 centrifugal-flow engine rated at 6,630lb (3,000kg) thrust.

To enable the MiG-15 to accommodate the VK-5, the main engine mount supporting struts were changed, the fuselage tail cone was modified, and a new extension pipe was installed. The aircraft was designated SL-5 by Mikoyan.

Upon completing development work, the aircraft was sent on 20 July 1951 for flight tests, which were carried out 15 August–31 October 1951. The centrifugal-flow engine was not further developed because the future belonged to axial-flow engines.

MiG-15bis (SE)

Following TsAGI recommendations, new wing tips were designed; simultaneously, the shape and area of the MiG-15 vertical tail surfaces were changed to improve controllability and to eliminate rudder reversal. Blueprints for these changes were issued in December 1950. Two prototypes, assigned the bureau designation SE, were completed in April 1951. Both went to the LII for tests carried out in June and July.

Tests revealed that the structural changes introduced into the SE did not resolve the roll reversal problem, so the program was canceled.

MiG-15bis (SDK-5) and SDK-7

During the late 1940s and early 1950s, a new trend originated at Mikoyan: a part of the bureau's efforts was directed to the creation of unmanned aircraft. Target aircraft and air-to-air missiles were designed for Tupolev long-range strategic bombers. Somewhat later, further programs for air-to-air missiles were initiated. Subsequently, teams developing unmanned aircraft formed separate organizations. They gave the VVS a great number of missiles, which formed the striking power of Soviet bombers.

The SDK-5 was a radio-controlled target aircraft based on the MiG-15bis. A few MiG-15s converted into targets were

The surveillance aerial of the RP-1 Izumrud radar was mounted in the upper air intake section, while the sighting aerial was placed in the air intake center body. The MiG-15bis (SP-5) prototype had two S-13 GSAP cameras, one installed at the windshield and another at the right side of the air intake.

The MiG-15bis (SP-5) prototype's armament included two NR-23 guns. The MiG-15bis (SP-5) nose fuselage structure was similar to the MiG-17P, MiG-17PF, MiG-19P, and MiG-19PM fighters, which were also equipped with the Izumrud-type radars.

One of two MiG-15bis (SE) flying test beds with modified empennage and wing tips.

MiG-15bis (SD-21) prototype with large-caliber ARS-212 (S-21) rockets.

MiG-15bis (SD-21) prototype with two external fuel tanks and two under-wing hardpoints.

58

used (together with the principal target aircraft, the La-17) during mock interceptions by Protivovozdushnaya Oborona (PVO; Air Defense Force—another branch of the Soviet military, responsible for air defense of the USSR) pilots.

During 1955, SDK-5s and SDK-7s (the latter also based on the MiG-15bis) were used to develop control systems for long-range air-launched missiles. Data obtained influenced the cruise missiles KS-10 (for the Tu-16K-10 bomber) and KSR-2 (for the Tu-16K-11-16), and other cruise missiles of the late 1950s.

MiG-15bis (SD-21)

The MiG-15bis (SD-21) was fitted with ARS-212 (S-21) rockets arranged in launcher pods on pylons. S-13 gun cameras were mounted aft of the pylons. The APU-0-212 launcher for the rockets was developed in April 1952. The launcher was suspended under the aircraft on type D3-40 carriers. With ARS-212 (S-21) rockets attached to the MiG-15bis, two 79gal (300ltr) external fuel tanks were retained. The new rockets underwent tests on the SD-21 and were used in fighter-bomber regiments of the VVS.

MiG-15bis (SD-5)

During November 1952, one SD-5 was created: a MiG-15bis fitted with two ORO-57 launch pods, each containing eight ARS-57 57mm rockets. These were attached to the wing pylons by D3-40 shackles, and AKS-2 gun cameras also fitted. Firing was electrically controlled. The SD-5 was never put into production.

MiG-15bis (SD-57)

In June 1952, a MiG-15bis was fitted with two D4-50 shackles to hold ORO-57 pods, each containing 12 ARS-57 rockets. This version was designated SD-57. The ARS-57s were widely used on

This 79gal (300ltr) external fuel tank and ARS-212 (S-21) rocket are mounted under a MiG-15bis (SD-21) wing.

later Soviet tactical aircraft.

MiG-15bis (SD-25)

The MiG-15bis version adapted to drop two PROSAB-250 antiaircraft bombs was designated SD-25. The bombs were attached via D4-50 shackles. In other respects, the aircraft did not differ from the production MiG-15bis. Smaller PROSAB-100 antiaircraft bombs designed to hit aircraft formations were used on the production aircraft.

MiG-15bis Attack and Fighter-Bomber Versions

After the end of the Great Patriotic War, Soviet attack air force units were

MiG-15bis (SD-57) prototype armed with two ORO-57 rocket pods, each with 12 ARS-57 rockets.

The MiG-15bis (ISh) attack fighter (ISh is the abbreviation for Istrebitel-Shturmovik, or Fighter-Attack Aircraft), exhibited at Monino Air Force Museum. The ISh had reinforced wings so that it could carry a large bomb load.

converted first to Il-10 attack aircraft and then to the Il-10M. Performance of these aircraft met requirements for close air support in the postwar era. The advent of jet fighters demanded development of more survivable high speed, close-air-support aircraft.

The concept of attack or *shturmovik* aircraft found ready acceptance in the USSR, and a number of prototype attack aircraft powered by piston, turbojet, and turboprop engines were produced, but by the early 1950s the VVS remained virtually without operational close-support

Top to bottom: a late production series MiG-15bis fighter equipped with OSP-48 blind landing system and armed with NR-23 guns; a MiG-15Rbis (SR) reconnaissance aircraft prototype with reduced armament comprising single N-37 and single NR-23 guns; a production MiG-15Rbis reconnaissance aircraft with standard armament; a MiG-15bis (ISh) attack fighter prototype; a MiG-15bis equipped for air-to-air refueling; and a MiG-15bis (SP-1) interceptor-fighter prototype equipped with Korshun radar.

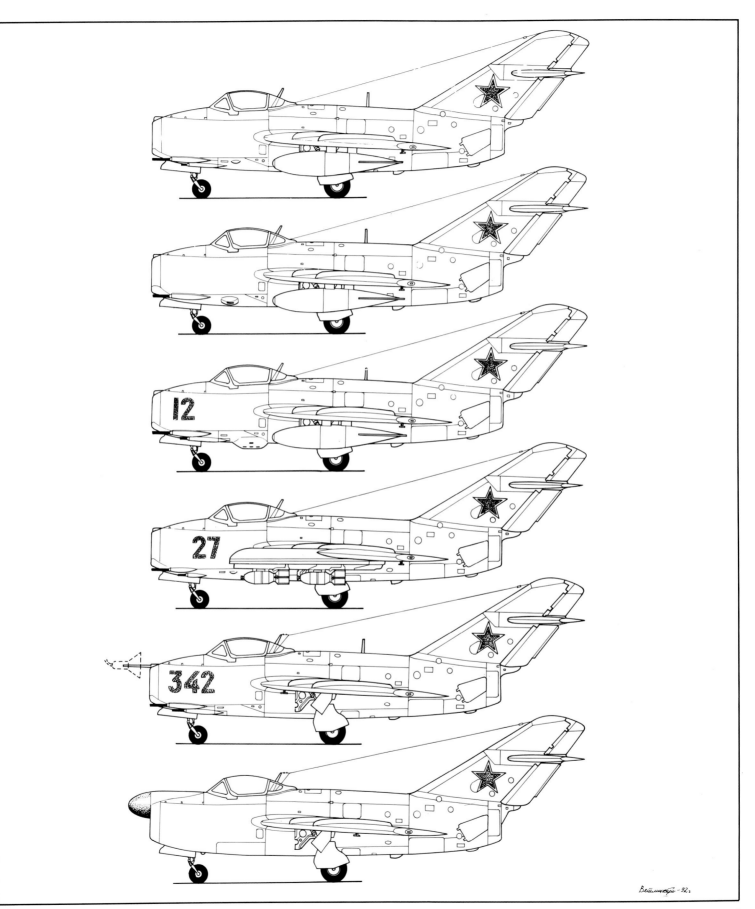

Only one MiG-15bis (ISh) was produced because the Sukhoi OKB was developing new designs for dedicated fighter-bomber aircraft.

The MiG-15bis (ISh) attack fighter's underwing bomb carriers were designed for this aircraft version.

aircraft. This gap was filled by rearming of attack units with MiG-15bis fighters. From 1957, these aircraft equipped fighter-bomber regiments of the VVS. From 1960, MiG-15bis were replaced in fighter-bomber units by Su-7B and MiG-17 aircraft.

As an attack aircraft and fighter-bomber, the MiG-15bis was limited by its modest bomb load of only two 45lb (100kg) bombs, and from absence of necessary navigation and weapons-delivery avionics, as well as poor armor protection, which consisted of canopy windshield armored glass, armor plate installed in front of the cockpit, and an armored headrest (an armored backrest was installed only on later versions). As a close-support aircraft, the MiG-15bis was powerfully armed with two 23mm and one 37mm guns. In addition, MiG-15bis ground-attack aircraft carried NURS 57mm rocket pods and powerful 212mm and 190mm rockets.

MiG-15bis (ISh) Fighter-Attack Version

To extend the combat capabilities of the MiG-15bis, Mikoyan in the early 1950s developed a new derivative, the MiG-15bis (ISh) fighter-attack airplane. The ISh differed from the basic version in having a reinforced wing and powerful weapon pylons for attachment of four 110–220lb (50–100kg) bombs or NURS rocket pods. It was also possible to suspend large-caliber rockets.

The MiG-15bis (ISh) was tested but not produced. Soviet doctrine called for a dedicated fighter-bomber. Aircraft of this type were developed by the Sukhoi OKB in the 1960s.

MiG-15bis Burlaki Long-Range Escort

In 1948 when Tu-4 long-range bombers entered service with the VVS, the problem arose of how to escort them. The USSR had never had escort fighters. Since an enemy could put aloft jet fighters capable of speeds nearly double that of the Tu-4, the heavy bomber's prospects for reaching its targets seemed low. This was the problem the Americans faced during the Korean War, where the American B-29 (from which the Tu-4 was copied) sustained heavy losses from MiG-15 fighters.

In the USSR, the Tu-83 long-range escort fighter was conceived but eventually canceled. There were no escort-

The forward fuselage of the MiG-15bis (ISh) was similar to that of the MiG-15.

The MiG-15bis (ISh) armament included one 37mm N-37 gun mounted on the right and two 23mm NR-23 guns on the left side.

The MiG-15bis (ISh) was capable of carrying two UB-8-57 rocket pods, each providing eight rockets, on underwing bomb carriers.

fighter modifications of Soviet interceptors. With its range of 1,565mi (2,520km), the MiG-15bis with 158gal (600ltr) external tanks could not escort Tu-4, with its 3,354mi (5,400km) range.

One way to the range problem was for the bombers to carry escort fighters with them. In the 1930s, a Soviet design team under V. Vakhmistrov tested "buddy" fighters carried piggyback atop a heavy bomber but this work was discontinued. In the United States after the Great Patriotic War, experiments were carried out with F-84 fighters towed by the B-29 and carried in the bay of the B-36. Created to develop an escort capabil-

ity, these projects led to reconnaissance, rather than escort, Republic RF-84K Thunderflash aircraft being carried in the bay of the B-36 in operational service.

A similar program was conducted in the early 1950s in the USSR. Responding to a Long Range Aviation Headquarters proposal, the Yakovlev OKB developed a system to enable the Tu-4 to tow MiG-15bis fighters. The system was code-named Burlaki.

A towing winch deployed a cable with special tips from the Tu-4. A clamp of "harpoon" type was mounted in the MiG-15bis forward fuselage. After take-off, the fighter caught the cable with its "harpoon." The MiG-15bis pilot shut his engine down and his aircraft was towed by the Tu-4 as a glider.

If enemy fighters attacked, the MiG-15bis pilot started his engine, disconnected from the rope, and went into combat. The system was tested and could

have been adopted, but not every pilot could stay in an unpressurized, unheated cockpit (with the engine off), wearing an oxygen mask for long hours. Worse, after air combat at its maximum range the fighter had little hope of reaching its home base if it became separated from the bombers.

Technology solved the problem. First, the Tu-4 was replaced by the Tu-16 jet bomber able to fly at 660mph (1,000km/h), or as fast as many fighters. Guns and ECM (electronic countermeasures) equipment gave the Tu-16 a good chance of reaching its target. Second, experiments began to provide fighters with AR (air-to-air refueling).

MiG-15bis With Aerial Refueling System

In the USSR, AR studies really began in 1948. In the 1930s, experiments in gravity-transfer of fuel from a higher to a ower aircraft were made with TB-1 and TB-3 bombers, but this method was not adopted. The revival of Russian interest in AR systems was prompted by the desire to increase the range of the Tu-4 and by the debut of jet aircraft with much higher fuel consumption than piston-engine airplanes.

A team headed by V. Vakhmistrov developed a system of "crossing ropes" (hoses) based on the Flight Refueling Limited hose apparatus adopted in the West. But this proved cumbersome, unreliable, and difficult to maintain. Worse, it required the tanker to stay directly above the receiver in formation flight.

A wing-to-wing AR system was developed by a team guided by test pilots I. Shelest and V. Vasyanin. Tests began, using the Tu-2 bomber, in the summer of 1949, and the system was adopted in service by Tu-4 units. The system later was used for Tu-16 bomber AR. In the 1950s, a "drogue" AR system was introduced on the Myasishchev 3M and Tu-95 heavy bombers, and later on the Tu-22 and Tu-22M supersonic long-range bombers. No system using a hard telescopic boom (like the US Air Force system) was developed because it would have required crew training and reliability standards that could not be achieved, in those days, in the USSR.

Development of AR techniques for front-line fighters and interceptors began at the same time as work on bomber AR, but Soviet designers did not create an effective fighter AR system until the 1980s. Four decades earlier, it seemed that the solution lay just a few years ahead.

Work on fighter AR systems took place at LII with active participation by the aircraft OKBs. The choice of AR scheme was dictated by the view that two fighters had to be able to refuel simultaneously.

Initially, a wing-to-wing AR system was tried. This scheme was tested using a Tu-2 tanker and Yak-15 receivers and later, in 1951, with MiG-15s. In one variant, a tanker pulled the loop formed by its hose and partially by rope and the fighter was equipped with a contact device and receptacle on its outer wing to seize the rope and connect to the hose tip. Contact was achieved by putting the fighter's outer wing down on the rope portion of the loop. The rope, seized by the contact unit, drove the hose tip to the receptacle.

Tests proved the potential for fast, reliable contact at high and low altitude, even in turbulence. The fighter's contact unit could be disconnected instantaneously and used for multiple contacts. The contact unit was small and could be installed on both outer wings for independent approach to the tanker. Despite all this, work on this system stopped. A system with two fighters employing drogues was deemed easier and worked faster.

Advantages offered by the drogue included simplicity of contact. An experimental drogue system was investigated using the Tu-4 tanker and two specially-equipped MiG-15s. The AR probe was installed on the front of the air intake on the left, forward fuselage. On contact, the MiG-15bis inserted its probe into the drogue, deployed from the tanker on a hose. Most modifications had to be made on the tanker. Two hoists with hoses were installed in the front bomb bay of the Tu-4. The hoses ran out to fairings on the wing tip. These hoses terminated with drogues protruding rearward from the tip fairings. Once the hoists were released, airflow forced the hoses to deploy. The system was tested at LII in 1953.

Designers were apprehensive about having the probe near the air-intake edge because they feared a stall at the air-intake lip. Flight testing put these fears to

The MiG-15bis during air-to-air refueling. The Soviet system uses an aircraft-mounted probe and a hose-mounted drogue dangled behind the tanker, similar to the system used by the US Navy. A Tupolev Tu-4 bomber (a reverse-engineered copy of the Boeing B-29) is used as a tanker.

Several MiG-15bis aircraft were modified for development of an air-to-air refueling system. The refueling probe was installed on the upper area of the forward fuselage.

A MiG-15bis converted for air-to-air refueling tests. This view shows the tapered probe mounted on the MiG's nose.

rest. However, several versions of the hose had to be tried before the system proved reliable. Even then, the fighter pilot found that just a little turbulence made the mid-air contact very difficult.

This combination of Tu-4 tanker and two MiG-15bis receivers was presented twice for official tests but failed both times because of problems with the hoists which, in turn, caused hose oscillation and breakage of the fighters' refueling probes.

During 1955–1956, work on fighter AR systems was continued with a MiG-19 test version, the SM-10, after which AR work was halted for a long time. In the 1960s, Soviet spending priorities went instead to missile development and production.

The first UTI-MiG-15 (ST-1) prototype during manufacturer's development tests.

UTI-MiG-15 (ST-1) and (ST-2)

On 16 April 1949, the Minister of Aircraft Industry ordered Mikoyan to design a trainer based on the MiG-15. The ST-1 (I-312) prototype aircraft was completed in May 1949 at plant No. 1 in Kuibyshev, primary manufacturer of the MiG-15.

The ST-1 differed from the MiG-15 in having tandem seating, with a front cockpit for a student pilot and a rear cockpit for the instructor. The aircraft had dual flight controls and armament of one NR-23 cannon and one 12.7mm (.50cal) UBK-E machine gun. An SPU-2M crew intercom was also installed. The front cockpit was rigged with a hinged canopy; the rear cockpit had a sliding canopy. Both parts of the canopy could be jetti-

The UTI-MiG-15 (ST-1) prototype was equipped with NR-23 23mm gun and .50cal (12.7mm) UBK-E machine gun. These were installed on the first aircraft prototype only.

A rear view of the first UTI-MiG-15 (ST-1) trainer prototype. All two-seaters were powered by the RD-45F turbojets and had air-brake panels similar to those of the production MiG-15 (SV) fighters.

The two-seat trainer version of the MiG-15, the UTI-MiG-15 (ST-1) Sparka, during official State flight tests at the Scientific and Research Institute of the Air Force airfield.

Two-seat cockpit of the Sparka prototype. The instructor sat in the rear cockpit, and the rear canopy slid back. The student sat in front, and the front canopy opened to the right.

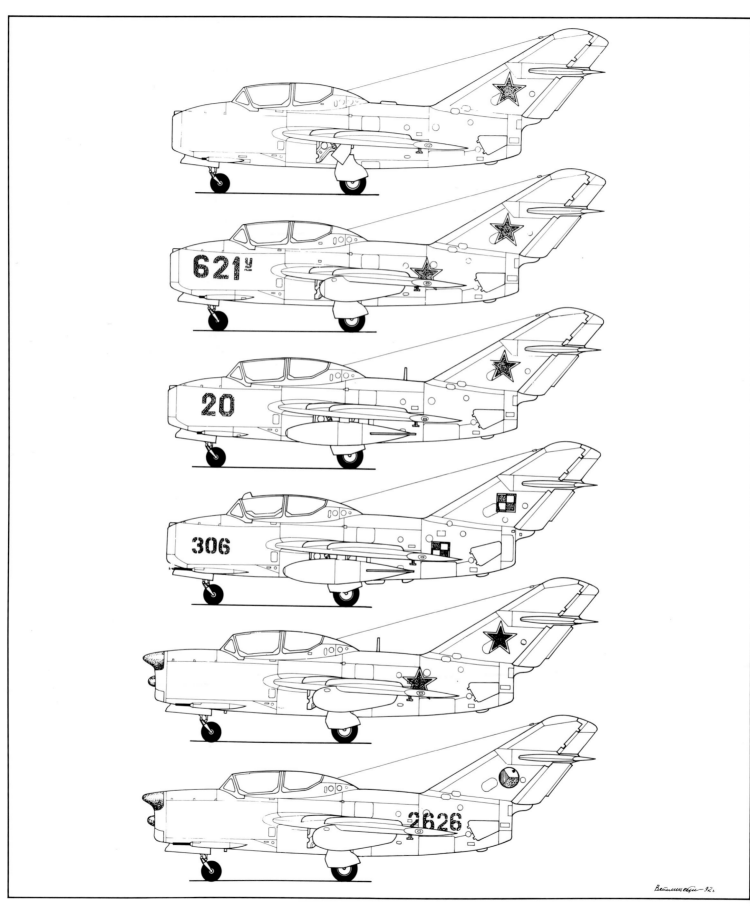

soned in an emergency manually or by means of explosive device. Landing gear and flaps could be retracted from either cockpit.

The ST-1's fuel system was also modified: a 25gal (95ltr) fuel tank was placed under the front cockpit, and a 201gal (760ltr) tank between frames 9 and 13, with the rear 71gal (268ltr) tank between frames 21 and 24. For longer flights, 66gal (250ltr) and 79gal (300ltr) external tanks could be installed.

Top to bottom: the first production UTI-MiG-15 (ST-1) trainer; a UTI-MiG-15 flying test bed with 66gal (250ltr) external fuel tanks; a production UTI-MiG-15 (ST-2) trainer with external fuel tanks; an SB Lim-2 two-seat trainer of the Polish air force; a UTI-MiG-15P (ST-7) two-seat trainer used for advanced training of pilots for the MiG-17P, MiG-17PF and MiG-19P interceptors equipped with the Izumrud radar; and a Czech-built version of the UTI-MiG-15 with RP-5 Izumrud radar.

Otherwise, the ST-1 was no different than the production MiG-15 (SV). An ASP-3N sight was installed in the front cockpit. This two-seat MiG-15 also had an RSI-6 two-way, short-wave (SW) radio, an RPK-10M radio direction finder, an AFA-IM camera, and an S-13 gun camera.

With this equipment the ST-1 underwent tests from 6 June to 18 August 1949. From 27 August to 29 September 1949, the ST-1 underwent state flight tests at NII VVS. From October 1949 to 1 April 1950, the ST-1 served with the fighter regiment at Kubinka air base near Moscow. In April, it was returned to the plant for maintenance. After 15 May 1950, the ST-1 was returned to NII VVS for engineering checks. After production testing in August 1950, the ST-1 was re-designated ST-2. Following further state testing, it was recommended for production.

The ST-2 became the standard for UTI-MiG-15 series production, but its de-

The UTI-MiG-15 two-seat combat trainer was capable of practically the same performance as the basic fighter from which it was derived.

sign and systems were continuously updated. In September 1953, a new 12.7mm A-12.7 machine gun replaced the UBK-E. A RSIU-3 UHF radio replaced the SW RSI-6. The ASP-3N sight gave way to the ASP-3NM with extended capacities. The SPU-2M intercom was mounted only in the instructor's cockpit. A Bary-M radar transponder was also installed. The UTI-MiG-15 trainer had to be constantly updated because there were no trainer versions of MiG-15bis, MiG-17, and MiG-19. A special UTI-MiG-15 was delivered to the Soviet cosmonauts' detachment to simulate transitory zero-G during training for manned space flight.

The UTI-MiG-15 was produced in large quantity at several plants. It was still operational in the 1970s, when it was fi-

71

UTI-MiG-15P (ST-7) prototype equipped with the RP-1 Izumrud radar. This two-seater was developed to allow Soviet pilots to master use of the Izumrud radar before having to use it in their single-seaters.

The ST-7 armament included a single .50cal (12.7mm) UBK-E machine gun. The aircraft front view shows the two Izumrud radar aerials.

Rear view of the UTI-MiG-15P (ST-7) undergoing manufacturer's development tests.

nally replaced by the MiG-21. After that it was used for a long time in the Voluntary Society for Support of the Soviet Army, Air Force, and Navy (DOSAAF, an organization that prepares Soviet youth for service with the armed forces) and for weather recon at flight schools and in combat units. The UTI-MiG-15 is still operational in third world countries.

UTI-MiG-15P (ST-7) and (ST-8)

To help Soviet pilots master the RP-1 Izumrud radar sight, two-seat MiG-15s were retrofitted with the Izumrud and designated ST-7. The ST-7 was armed with one UBK-E 12.7mm (.50cal) machine gun. After testing and production, a small batch of them was delivered to combat units as UTI-MiG-15P aircraft.

The advanced RP-3 Izumrud-3 sight was fitted to a UTI-MiG-15 in 1955 and the aircraft was designated ST-8. The ST-

This flying test bed based on the UTI-MiG-15 (call number 101ᵧ) was intended for ejection seat tests.

In-flight testing of the front ejection seat on a UTI-MiG-15.

Rear ejection seat testing on a UTI-MiG-15 flying laboratory, call number 102^y.

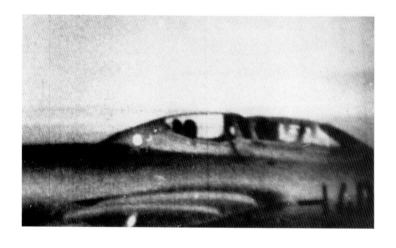

This shot shows testing of the SK ejection seat system, developed for the MiG-21 fighter program. For this purpose, the front cockpit of the UTI-MiG-15 flying test bed was equipped with a MiG-21 canopy.

This shot shows how the pilot was protected by the canopy immediately after ejection from the UTI-MiG-15. This ejection seat system, designated SK, was used on early MiG-21s.

8 differed from the production UTI-MiG-15 in many subtle ways, including removal of the front fuel tank, use of modified forward fuselage section as on the MiG-15Pbis, adding a radar power supply, and reinforcing the nose landing gear.

The Izumrud-3 radar, tested on the ST-8, became the basis for the RP-5 radar later used on the MiG-17P interceptor.

UTI-MiG-15 (ST-10)

Pilots were often injured in high-speed ejections because first-generation ejection seats offered no protection from the wind blast after ejection and the seats were not stabilized, so they tumbled in the slipstream, adding to the likelihood of pilot injury. The VVS examined several means of increasing the chance of safe egress at high-speed, including enclosed ejection capsules, but decided that improved ejection seats were the least expensive, simplest, and lightest solution to the problem.

An experimental rig was used in tests

Top to bottom: three versions of the UTI-MiG-15 based flying test beds intended for SK ejection seat development; this UTI-MiG-15 (ST-10) flying test bed was used for testing of the first version of the SK ejection seat system with a canopy that protected the pilot; and a diagram showing how the canopy ejected with the seat to protect the pilot (the seat was later applied to early production versions of MiG-21 fighters).

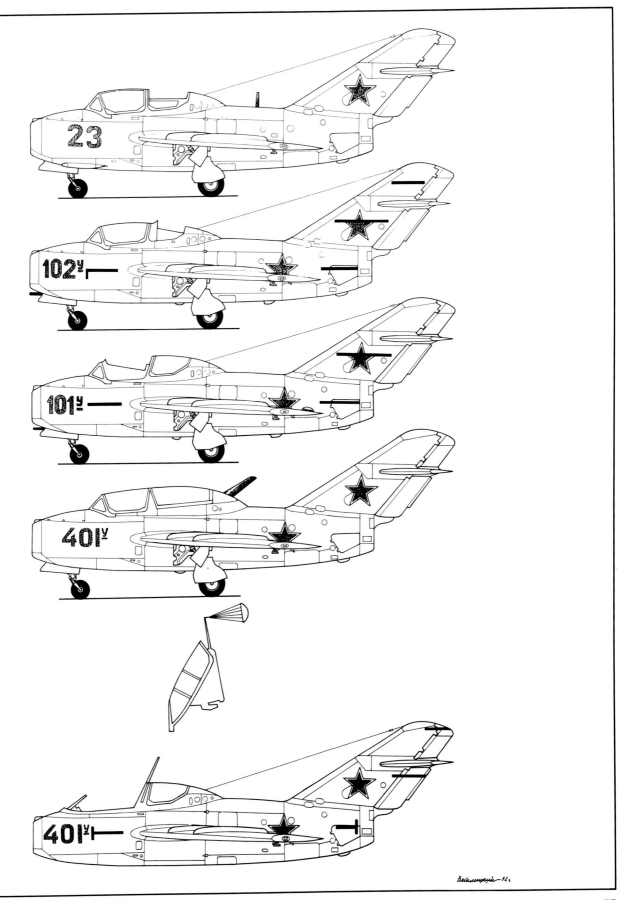

A flying test bed converted from the UTI-MiG-15. The rear cockpit, intended for installation of different ejection seats, has no canopy at all.

The moment of ejection, with a mannequin or "dummy pilot." Thousands of similar experiments were performed before ejection-seat systems were mature enough to pass official State tests and to be introduced into production.

ejecting a dummy at up to 621mph (1,000km/h). New stabilizing devices for the seat were investigated. In ground tests, actual pilots were ejected with a canopy used as a screen for protection. These first tests were conducted on Tu-2 aircraft.

In 1954, an experimental ejection system was placed in the rear cockpit of a UTI-MiG-15 aircraft for conducting ejection-seat tests with both dummies and pilots. This version of the MiG-15 was designated ST-10.

Weights up to 497lb (225kg) were ejected. An explosive charge provided ejection speed of about 61ft/sec (18.5m/sec). Tests were conducted in the late 1950s. Several stabilizing systems were investigated while testing, among them a seat stabilizing system using a parachute. Testing was conducted by pilot E. Yelyan and parachutist Golovin. As a result, an ejection mount with a sliding canopy was recommended for pilot protection from the airflow for all Soviet fighters capable of exceeding 660mph (1,000km/h).

UTI-MiG-15 trainers were built in large quantities, especially in Poland and Czechoslovakia, and served with the Soviet Air Force for many years.

MiG-15 two-seaters undergoing a preflight turnaround.

Soviet Air Force Higher Military Pilot Schools were first to receive the production UTI-MiG-15. Cadets gained pilot skills and experience flying the UTI-MiG-15s.

Each cadet had to perform a number of familiarization and training flights before his first solo flight.

A Military Pilot School instructor occupies the rear cockpit of the UTI-MiG-15. Soviet Air Force instructor pilots usually had over 1,000 flying hours.

This military cadet is happy after a successful solo flight.

A production UTI-MiG-15 with two 66gal
(250ltr) external fuel tanks.

A technician inspecting an aircraft during
preflight preparations. Technicians considered
the UTI-MiG-15 to be very simple and reliable,
both in maintenance and operation.

UTI-MiG-15s were operational with the Soviet Air Force until the mid-1960s, when new two-seater combat trainers such as the Mikoyan MiG-21U and Sukhoi Su-7U and Su-9U were introduced into the Soviet Air Force inventory.

The UTI-MiG-15 cockpit had a side-hinged forward canopy and a sliding rear canopy.

Production UTI-MiG-15s were armed with a single .50cal (12.7mm) machine gun. This was conventional for Soviet Air Force two-seaters.

The capability of the aircraft to carry two 106gal (400ltr) external tanks increased endurance and improved the effectiveness of training.

The rear cockpit of a Soviet Air Force combat unit's UTI-MiG-15 was often empty when the aircraft was used for solo training of combat pilots.

UTI-MiG-15s are on display in most Soviet pilot school museums. This was the first jet plane flown by many Soviet pilots.

A UTI-MiG-15 Sparka taxies by a more modern MiG-21 for takeoff from a Soviet airfield in the 1960s.

Some UTI-MiG-15s were transferred to the DOSAAF, where they were used for training of sportsmen-pilots in flying jet aircraft.

A DOSAAF UTI-MiG-15 equipped with two 66gal (250ltr) external tanks.

A number of Soviet aero clubs had UTI-MiG-15s. Not only sportsmen, but Soviet Air Force cadets flew these two-seaters. Later, they were replaced by Czech-built L-29 Delphin and L-39 Albatross trainers.

The MiG-15 became the pride of the Soviet aircraft industry. One can see monuments devoted to this aircraft all over the country, not only in towns where the military pilot schools are located, but in many Soviet Air Force units.

At right and next page
A number of UTI-MiG-15 two-seaters were converted into the flying test beds for research programs and experiments. Aircraft of this category usually had three-digit call numbers and followed by a small superscript У, as on these test beds $412^У$, $501^У$, and $621^У$.

Chapter 3

MiG-15s Outside the Soviet Union

Czechoslovakian MiG-15 Production

A decision to produce the MiG-15 in Czechoslovakia was made in 1950. Some aircraft from Russian-supplied parts received the Czech designation S-102. Production of the MiG-15 was assigned to the Rudy Letov plant at Letnany. First tests of a Czech-produced MiG-15 began in 1952. Production of the MiG-15 began at Aero, a new plant in Vodochody. The first Czech-built MiG-15 flew on 28 April 1953. Production continued into 1954 and 853 MiG-15s were produced by Aero. The MiG-15bis version, or Czech S-103, went into production in 1954, and 620 were built. From 1956, the UTI-MiG-15 trainer, or Czech CS-102, was built at Aero, the total number reaching no fewer than 2,012 aircraft.

Production of RD-45F (Czech M-05) and VK-1 (Czech M-06) engines began at Motorlet in 1952. The plant turned out 5,000 engines, which powered Czech MiG-15, MiG-15bis, and Il-28 aircraft.

Czech MiG-15bis were delivered to Egypt and Syria in 1955–1956 and UTI-MiG-15s went to nearly all countries with MiG-15, MiG-17, and MiG-19 fighters. In fact, Czechoslovakia became the biggest UTI-MiG-15 producer outside the USSR.

Some Czech MiG-15 and MiG-15bis fighters were reequipped as target-towing aircraft and designated MiG-15T and MiG-15bisT. Guns were removed, and a cable system for target-tow work was installed.

The Czech MiG-15bisF versions, also called "Photobis," were developed for tactical reconnaissance. This modification had an AFA-1M or AFP-21KT aerial camera installed in place of guns.

More redesigning was needed for the MiG-15bisR version. Together with the AFP-21KT, two additional cameras were installed inside the fuselage while internal fuel was reduced. Armament of one 23mm gun was retained. For night photo reconnaissance a NFT-02 camera was mounted on MiG-15bisR.

Some MiG-15bis and UTI-MiG-15 aircraft were retrofitted with the PPZ-1 landing-control system designed in Czechoslovakia. The system's aerial was installed in a fairing in the upper inlet.

In 1958, modification of Czech MiG-15s for the fighter-bomber mission began,

Almost 1,500 MiG-15 and MiG-15bis single-seat fighters were built in Czechoslovakia. Many of these were still operational 20 years after production began. The MiG-15s were designated S-102 and were built at the Rudy Letov and Aero factories from 1952 to 1954. The Czech-produced MiG-15bis was designated S-103 and went into production in 1954. This S-103 is exhibited in a Czech museum.

Top to bottom: a UTI-MiG-15 intended for the SK ejection seat development program; a Czech air force MiG-15 SB with PPZ-1 landing system; a MiG-15bis of the Czech air force aerobatic team; MiG-15Rbis from Czech air force Ostrava-based fighter bomber regiment; a Czech air force MiG-15bis that was used as an adversary aircraft during tactical exercises (note blue stripes on the fuselage sides and fin); and a MiG-15 of the Czech air force aerobatic team of the early 1950s.

Czech-produced MiG-15bis were exported to Egypt and Syria in 1955–1956.

In late 1956, the Aero factory began production of the UTI-MiG-15 trainer, designated CS-102. The Sparkas were manufactured in large quantities and exported to several countries, including the Soviet Union, which by that time had switched production to the MiG-17. Czechoslovakia became the main manufacturer of the UTI-MiG-15 outside the Soviet Union. Among more than 7,000 MiG-15s built, approximately 30 percent were Czech-built Sparkas.

the new version being designated MiG-15SB. This aircraft was fitted for missiles and bombs, with six pylons instead of the usual two, and the guns were retained. Normal takeoff weight of this version was 12,875lb (5,826kg), and the maximum reached 13,857lb (6,270kg). To take off from short or unpaved runways, two SRP-1 solid-propellant booster rockets were used. Landing roll was reduced by a braking parachute. Typical ordnance loads included four R-130 missiles or four SR-55 rocket projectile pods, with 106gal (400ltr) fuel tanks on the middle hardpoints.

The MiG-15bisSB came in 1968. Ordnance was identical to the MiG-15SB, but booster rockets and brake parachute were deleted. Normal and maximum takeoff weights were slightly increased. A project to retrofit the MiG-15bisSB with K-13 air-to-air missiles was carried out for the North Vietnamese air force. Missiles occupied the pylons otherwise used by fuel tanks. The 37mm gun was replaced with an infrared target detection system. After one airframe underwent production tests, work on the project was halted.

Some Czech MiG-15bis, as in the USSR, were rebuilt into flying targets with remote-control systems. One UTI-MiG-15 was used in development of the ejection seat for the L-39 trainer.

In 1959, the Czech defense ministry ordered one UTI-MiG-15 retrofitted for Izumrud-5 (RP-5) radar installation, which became standard equipment for the MiG-17P and PF. This aircraft was called the UTI-MiG-15P. Intended for radar training of fighter pilots, it was identical to the Soviet ST-8 version except for the radar type. The radar display was installed in the rear cockpit. Weight of the aircraft was increased slightly as compared to the basic trainer but performance was basically unchanged. Range and endurance dropped slightly due to reduction of fuel capacity by 7.7 percent in the internal tanks. The UTI-MiG-15P was not produced in Czechoslovakia. The only Czech-produced example is preserved today at the Museum of Aircraft and Cosmonautics in the Czech Republic.

Many Czech UTI-MiG-15s were exported to the USSR and served the VVS for a long period. Later, they were turned over to DOSAAF. According to pilots, UTI-MiG-15 aircraft from Czechoslovakia were more carefully produced than their Soviet counterparts, due to the skill of workers and engineers and the high level of European technology.

UTI-MiG-15 aircraft produced in Czechoslovakia were also used in the USSR for cosmonaut training. This was the aircraft on which the first cosmonaut, Y. Gagarin, and pilot-instructor V. Seryegin were killed in an accident on 27 March 1968.

Polish MiG-15 Production

In 1951 the MiG-15 began gearing up for production in Poland's WSK plant in Melets. RD-45F engines were manufactured at the WSK plant in Zhehuv. Production of the MiG-15 benefitted not just the aviation field but all of heavy industry in Poland, nurturing a highly-skilled cadre of workers and engineers.

On 17 July 1952, test-pilot Major ˹nevsky performed the maiden flight of ˹e Polish MiG-15, assembled from So-˹iet parts. Poland designated the aircraft ˹im-1 and the RD-45F engine Lis-1. An ˹nitial batch of six Lim-1s (nos. 1A-˹01/1A-006) was produced in 1952.

Full-scale production of the Lim-1 ˹asted from January 1953 to 1 September ˹954. Twelve batches were built, totaling ˹27.

Late in 1953, production of the MiG-˹5bis and VK-1A engine began. The first ˹olish MiG-15bis, called the Lim-2 (no. ˹B-001) was rolled out on 17 September ˹954. Its Polish VK-1A engine was desig-˹ated Lis-2. The latest MiG-15bis with ˹SP-48, Bary-M IFF, and landing light in ˹he left wing was produced beginning in ˹956. In all, 500 Lim-2 aircraft were pro-˹uced in 19 batches. The last Lim-2 (no. ˹B 019-14), was manufactured on 11 No-˹ember 1956. Meanwhile, Lim-1 fighters ˹ere upgraded with avionics identical to ˹he Lim-2s and were redesignated Lim-˹.5. Some Lim-2s were produced as Lim-˹2R reconnaissance aircraft. In these, an ˹FA-21 camera was installed behind the ˹23mm guns in a special container.

UTI-MiG-15s were not manufactured ˹n Poland, but were delivered from the ˹USSR and Czechoslovakia. But because ˹f an urgent need for trainers in the Pol-˹sh air force in the late 1950s, some Lim-˹s were rebuilt to become SB Lim-1 oper-˹ational trainers. The SB Lim-1 had minor ˹equipment differences from UTI-MiG-˹15s.

In the 1970s, Poland's supply of Lis-1 ˹engines was exhausted. In 1975, Lim-2s ˹ere rebuilt into SB Lim-2 trainers using ˹Lis-2 engines. The SB Lim-2 had just one ˹23mm gun.

Some of these two-seaters were ˹adapted for reconnaissance. These were ˹designated SB Lim-1A and SB Lim-2A ˹(initial designations SB Lim-1Art and SB ˹Lim-2Art). The SB Lim-1A had an AFA-˹21A camera, while the SB Lim-2A had ˹two cameras, AFA-21 and AFA-39.

Some SB Lim-2As were converted to ˹SB Lim-2M trainers after years of opera-˹tional use. Armament remained two ˹23mm guns.

Some MiG-15s in Poland were used ˹as flying laboratories. One Soviet-built ˹MiG-15bis was used by the Polish Air-˹craft Institute for investigation of aerody-˹namic configurations of new aircraft de-˹signed in Poland. This work contributed

A CS-102 of the Czech Ostravsky fighter-bomber regiment in flight.

to the TS-11 Iskra aircraft and meteoro-logical rockets of the 1960s.

Production of the Lim-1 and Lim-2 gave valuable experience to the Polish aircraft industry which later produced the MiG-17, beginning in 1956. The Lim-1 and Lim-2 were not exported.

Chinese MiG-15 Production

In March 1950, the Chinese govern-ment decided that China should build modern jet aircraft. The USSR, as an "older brother," immediately proffered help. In October 1951 (after Chinese and other pilots had already been flying So-viet-built MiG-15s in combat for a year), 847 Soviet specialists traveled to China to arrange production of the MiG-15bis at China's Shenyang aircraft complex. As it turned out, the Chinese moved directly to production of the MiG-17 (in 1956) and

Poland was one of the first countries to receive the MiG-15 for its air force. Having gotten the license for the MiG-15 production, Poland began producing them at the WSK plant in 1952. Polish MiG-15s were designated Lim-1.

never built the MiG-15bis. But during the Korean War, 534 battle-damaged MiG-15s and MiG-15bis were repaired at Shenyang. The UTI-MiG-15 two-seater *was* produced in China and delivered to Albania, Bangladesh, North Korea, Pak-istan, Tanzania, and North Vietnam. MiG-15s aircraft were still operational in China in the early 1970s.

The MiG-15bis was given the Chi-nese designation J-2 (export designation F-2). The UTI-MiG-15 produced in China was called the JJ-2 (export designation FT-2).

A Polish Lim-1 during takeoff.

The Polish Lim-1 entered production in July 1952. Full-scale production of these aircraft began in January 1953.

License production of the Polish-built Lim-1 lasted until September 1954, by which time 227 had been built.

A Polish pilot and his technicians pose with their Lim-1 as the background.

The Polish version of the Soviet MiG-15bis was designated Lim-2. The first Lim-2 was completed in September 1954.

Production of the Lim-2 lasted until November 1956. Approximately 500 were delivered.

A Polish air force MiG-15 undergoing routine maintenance.

A part of the Lim-2 fleet included the photographic-reconnaissance version, designated Lim-2R. An AFA-21 reconnaissance pod was mounted behind the NR-23 guns on the Lim-2R.

One of the Polish Aviation Institute's flying test beds based on the MiG-15.

A Polish Lim-2R.

*A Lim-2 in the Museum of Combat
Brotherhood in Drzonov.*

This Polish MiG-15bis is now a part of exhibition at the Polish Armed Forces Museum in Warsaw.

The UTI-MiG-15 was not manufactured in Poland. These aircraft were imported from the Soviet Union and Czechoslovakia. Some MiG-15 single-seaters were converted into the UTI-MiG-15s, designated SB Lim-1s, at Polish aircraft plants.

By 1975, the Polish air force was out of Polish-built RD-45F engines (designated Lis-1), so they converted Lim-2s into two-seat trainers, designated SB Lim-2.

License built two-seaters and single-seat fighters as well were continuously retrofitted. This photo shows one of the modifications of the trainer, designated SB Lim-2M.

The Polish version of the photographic-reconnaissance MiG was designated SB Lim-2R. Photographic equipment is installed in a fuselage-mounted pod.

The photographic pod of the SB Lim-2R was mounted under the center fuselage.

*A Polish SB Lim-1 two-seater undergoing
routine maintenance. The removed rear
fuselage reveals the Lis-1 turbojet.*

*One of the Polish Sparkas was used as a flying
test bed for aerodynamic research for the I-22
Irida aircraft.*

This SB Lim-2 two-seater is exhibited in the Krakow Air Force Museum.

This Polish SB Lim-1 with call number 1018 was used as a flying laboratory for ejection-seat development and for training pilots in emergency procedures.

The SB Lim-1 flying laboratory in flight, seconds before the ejection of the pilot from the rear cockpit.

The moment of ejection from the SB Lim-1 flying laboratory.

Top to bottom: the only Czech air force UTI-MiG-15 equipped with RP-1 Izumrud radar; 2 Polish-built Lim-2R reconnaissance aircraft with photographic equipment; the Lim-2 was the Polish version of the later production series MiG-15bis; the SB Lim-2 is the two-seat combat trainer version of the Lim-2 single-seater; a North Korea MiG-15bis of the 64th Fighter Air Corps (FAC), painted in a camouflage scheme was introduced since 1952; and a former Chinese Navy MiG-15bis (J-2) now in the United States, registered No. 15M6, in a paint scheme similar to that of Soviet MiG-15s of the 324th Fighter Air Division, which participated in Korean operations in spring and summer of 1951.

Белоцкий 92.

MiG-15 In Service With Other Nations

Afghanistan: In 1957, the USSR delivered a MiG-17B and three UTI-MiG-15s to Afghanistan. The UTI-MiG-15s were used to train pilots of the Afghan air force. In the 1980s, they were still operational alongside Czech L-39 trainers.

Albania: In 1950, the first Soviet MiG-15 went into service with the Albanian air forces. Two squadrons of MiG-15s were formed that year, based near Tirana. Later these Albanian aircraft were used as fighter-bombers. Also in the 1950s, UTI-MiG-15s were delivered to Albania. In the early 1960s due to the rupture of diplomatic relations with the USSR, Albania began receiving Chinese F-2s and FT-2s. In the mid-1980s, one squadron of F-2 and some FT-2 aircraft were still operational.

Algeria: Early in 1963, the first Soviet MiG-15bis and UTI-MiG-15 fighters were delivered to Algeria. These aircraft formed a fighter-bomber regiment, consisting of three squadrons and intended for close air support. Some were delivered via Egypt. In 1984, 20 MiG-15bis and UTI-MiG-15 aircraft were still operational in Algeria and used for training pilots.

Angola: In the mid-1980s, two UTI-MiG-15s delivered from the USSR were still operational with the Angola air force.

Bulgaria: The first jet fighter in Bulgaria, beginning in July 1950, was the Yak-23. It was not operational for long and soon MiG-15bis and UTI-MiG-15s, delivered from the USSR, formed two air regiments. MiG-15s were used as fighter-bombers. In the mid-1980s, only a few UTI-MiG-15 aircraft were still operational in the Bulgarian air forces.

Cambodia: Chinese MiG-15bis and UTI-MiG-15s (F-2s and FT-2s) were delivered to Cambodia during the reign of Prince Norodom Sihanouk. None survives today.

China: The first Soviet jet fighters began serving in China in 1950. These were Yak-17 UTI and MiG-9 trainers. Soviet instructors also came to China. From the beginning of the war in Korea, Chinese pilots began intensive training in the USSR for combat in the MiG-15. In spring 1951, the first Chinese pilots took part in air combats in Korea. The loss rate of MiG-15s flown by Chinese pilots was high because they were inexperienced and were fighting experienced American

opponents, many of whom had been aces in the Great Patriotic War. Moreover, many accidents took place while taking off and landing. Even worse, Chinese pilots often lost consciousness in high-g maneuvers because food was strictly rationed, with the result that these pilots were chronically malnourished. The results were deplorable. The overall 8:1 kill ratio of combats between the F-86 and MiG-15 mostly reflects combat of American and Chinese pilots. The kill ratio of combat between American and Soviet pilots in Korea was, from the Soviet viewpoint, equal.

During the war in Korea, mass deliveries of the MiG-15 and MiG-15bis took place from the USSR to China. These continued after the war. The UTI-MiG-15 was also delivered to China before being put into licence production. Early in the 1960s, all MiG-15bis (J-2s) were converted into fighter-bombers. At that time more than 200 J-2 aircraft were serving in China. Some were exported and by the mid-1980s only 90 J-2s and 300 JJ-2s were still operational in China.

Cuba: Deliveries of aircraft from the USSR to Cuba began after Fidel Castro came to power. The Cuban air force received a few MiG-15bis. These aircraft did not take part in the April 1961 combat actions at the Bay of Pigs because the Cubans had only ten pilots, trained in out-of-date American aircraft. When MiG-17s and MiG-19s went into service, UTI-MiG-15s were delivered from the USSR. By the middle of the 1980s, only 20 UTI-MiG-15s were still operational in Cuba.

Czechoslovakia: The first Czechoslovakian pilots mastered the MiG-15, guided by Soviet instructors, as early as 1951. By 1953, some Czechoslovakian air regiments were already converted to the new aircraft. MiG-15s were delivered from the USSR first, then placed into production at Aero. The same happened with the UTI-MiG-15 trainer.

In the spring of 1953, a pair of Czechoslovakian MiG-15s shot down an American F-84 that had crossed the Czech frontier. A year later, one more trespasser was shot down by Czech MiG-15bis aircraft. It was the time of Cold War between East and West, a time of looking at one another through gun sights. From 1954 to 1965, Czech MiG-15s aircraft often intercepted balloons carrying reconnaissance equipment and printed materi-

als. The total number of such objects launched eastward was up to 150,000. The interception of these balloons was difficult because a balloon is a very weak radar target and had to be acquired visually. The skin of the balloons was sectional, and even a direct hit might not bring it down. It was necessary to shoot down the balloons for two reasons: first, they could survey secrets, and second, they could deliver the West's subversive literature. Even more dangerous was the risk of collision with civil and military aircraft. Fighting the balloons became most important for pilots of the Warsaw Pact during that period.

MiG-15 and MiG-15bis fighter-bombers were operational in the Czechoslovakian air force as late as the 1970s when they were replaced by Su-7s and Su-22s. The MiG-15bis was still operational in the early 1980s.

Egypt: The first delivery of the MiG-15bis from Czechoslovakia to Egypt was made in 1955. During the 1956 Suez crisis, most were destroyed on the ground or simply failed to take part in combat actions. After 1956, more advanced MiG-17s and MiG-19s went to Egypt, together with UTI-MiG-15s to supplement those provided earlier. During the 1967 Six-Day War, the MiG-15bis was perhaps the only fighter-bomber operating over Israeli army positions. Again, however, most were destroyed on the ground, demonstrating to the world the that Arab forces were weak and their Soviet sponsors were throwing money away. The MiG-15 was replaced at first by more modern Soviet aircraft in the 1970s, and later by Western types.

Finland: In the 1970s, four UTI-MiG-

Top to bottom: a Hungarian air force MiG-15bis equipped with the OSP-48 blind landing system; an early production series MiG-15bis with OSP-48 blind landing system. It was used in the Hungarian air force as a fighter-bomber; a Cuban air force MiG-15bis equipped with the OSP-48 blind landing system; a former Polish SB Lim-2 (manufacturer's code 1A-06-038) that was imported to the United States and was used by the Defense Test and Evaluation Agency at Kirkland Air Force Base, New Mexico; one of the American, privately-owned MiG-15bis; and a Polish Lim-2 (manufacturer's code 1B-01-205, civil registration number N205JM), used in Steal the Sky, *a TV movie.*

UTI-MiG-15s operated by the Finnish air force.

15s with the latest equipment, including the Bary-M, OSP-48, and landing light in the wing, were still operational in the Finland air force.

Germany: The MiG-15bis and UTI-MiG-15 were the first jet fighters in service with East Germany. Training of pilots and technical personnel was largely conducted in the USSR. The first aircraft were delivered in 1956. They became an important part of the Soviet military group in Germany. There were only a few MiG-15bis in the German air force, and beginning in 1958, they were replaced by

MiG-17F fighters. The UTI-MiG-15 was still operational in the 1970s.

Guinea: In the 1960s, the USSR helped Guinea to organize an air force with a squadron of MiG-17Fs and UTI-MiG-15 trainers.

Hungary: Hungary, as a front-line country in the struggle with imperialism, was among the first to receive the MiG-15, known locally as the Jaguar. Plans for production of the MiG-15 at the plant in Adiliget were interrupted by the 1956 Hungarian uprising. MiG-15bis and UTI-MiG-15s were also delivered from the USSR and Czechoslovakia. The MiG-15bis was for a time operational in Hungary as a fighter-bomber. The UTI-MiG-15 is still flown in Hungary today.

Indonesia: Late in the 1950s and early in the 1960s, the Soviet "flow" of armament reached Indonesia. That island country received during a short time a *Sverdlov*-class light cruiser, two squadrons of Tu-16KS bombers with KS-1 Kometa air-to-surface cruise missiles, and a squadron of MiG-21F-13s with the best Soviet pilots from the air regiment in Kubinka. UTI-MiG-15s were also sent to Indonesia to train pilots for the MiG-17 and MiG-19, which were also delivered to that country. After General Suharto came to power in 1965, relations with the USSR changed dramatically. By 1965, most Soviet personnel and equipment were withdrawn, while remaining equipment became inoperable due to the absence of spares. Later, Indonesia used only arms from the West.

Iraq: After the downfall of the monarchy and establishment the revolutionary Casem regime in Iraq in 1958, MiG-15bis, UTI-MiG-15, and MiG-17 aircraft were delivered. In the 1960s, a squadron of MiG-15bis fighter-bombers was formed. There was also a squadron of UTI-MiG-15 trainers. In the mid-1980s, a few UTI-MiG-15s were still operational in the Iraqi air force.

Libya: After another great "socialist," Muamar Khaddafi, came to power, Soviet weapons were rushed to Libya. Delivery of modern aircraft began in the 1970s, but a few UTI-MiG-15s remained in service to prolong the service life of more expensive combat trainers delivered from the USSR.

Malagasy Republic: After independence, Madagascar received standard Soviet "humanitarian help": the MiG-17 and UTI-MiG-15 fighters.

Mali: During the period of friendship between the USSR and Mali, some MiG-17 and UTI-MiG-15 were delivered to that country.

Mongolia: In the mid-1980s, Mongolia had some 150 aircraft, including MiG-15bis. Today, only UTI-MiG-15s remain operational.

Morocco: In the 1960s, the kingdom of Morocco purchased 20 MiG-17s and two UTI-MiG-15s. Later, Morocco bought US and French aircraft.

Mozambique: In addition to the MiG-17, Mozambique received some UTI-MiG-15s.

Nigeria: During its war with Biafra, Nigeria received some UTI-MiG-15s. By the mid-1980s only two were still operational.

North Korea: North Korea went to war in June 1950 with about 150 Soviet aircraft of Great Patriotic War vintage. Almost immediately, the North Korean air force was completely destroyed by United Nations (UN) allies, but after Russia's intervention (November 1950), the North Korean air arm was created anew with deliveries of Soviet MiG-15s. Deliveries were so great to Chinese and Russian combat units and losses so imposing that the USSR was forced to reduce the pace of its rearmament in Europe.

After the end of the war in July 1953, the North Korean air force had an inventory of several hundred of MiG-15bis. The MiG-15bis remained a first-line fighter up to the late 1950s, when they were gradually replaced by more modern Soviet and later Chinese aircraft. The UTI-MiG-15 remained operational in training squadrons in North Korea up to the 1980s.

North and South Yemen: Both countries, allies of the USSR, received MiGs. Today, only some UTI-MiG-15s remain. The supplier never imagined that aircraft of these neighboring countries would meet in air combat during a border conflict.

North Vietnam: Vietnam received weapons from both the USSR and China, employing both Soviet- and Chinese-built MiG-15s. A squadron of UTI-MiG-15s remained operational in the mid-1980s.

Pakistan: When Pakistan began military ties with China, it received F-2 and FT-2 export fighters. These have since been discarded.

Poland: Polish air force fighter regiments began rearming with the MiG-15 in 1951. The Warsaw Air Regiment was first. Early Polish MiG-15s were delivered from the USSR, but later combat units began to receive Polish-built versions. The first Polish Lim-1 went into service late in 1952. In 1953, delivery of the MiG-15bis began from the USSR and in late 1954 the first Lim-2 went into service.

Poland received two-seaters from Czechoslovakia. Various MiG-15s formed the basis of the Polish air force for a long period and in the 1970s the MiG-15bis was still serving as a fighter-bomber. UTI-MiG-15s still served in the 1980s.

Rumania: In Rumania, as in Bulgaria, the MiG-15 replaced the Yak-23 in the early 1950s. The MiG-15bis served as a fighter-bomber in the Rumanian air force

A phased-out Hungarian air force MiG-15 exhibited at an air force museum.

until the mid-1980s, when more than 40 UTI-MiG-15 aircraft were still operational in Rumania.

Sri Lanka (Ceylon): In the 1960s, Sri Lanka received MiG-17s and one UTI-MiG-15 from the USSR. These were still operational in the 1980s.

Somalia: In the 1960s, Somalia also received MiGs from the USSR. The MiG-15bis were used as fighter-bombers. Two UTI-MiG-15s were still operational in the 1980s.

Sudan: After the establishment of Nimairy regime, Sudan's air force received Soviet aircraft, including the UTI-MiG-15.

Syria: Syria had received its first MiG-15bis from Czechoslovakia in 1956. Later came further deliveries, including UTI-MiG-15s. Syria's MiG-15s took part in all Middle East conflicts, but most were destroyed on the ground, not in air combat. Only one squadron of UTI-MiG-15s was still operational by the mid-1980s.

Tanzania: Tanzania received weapons from China, including two F-2s still operational in the mid-1980s.

Uganda: Two UTI-MiG-15s and some MiG-17s served in Uganda.

The West and the MiG-15

When a MiG-15 prototype flew over Tushino airfield during the air parade in

July 1948, Western intelligence experts gave little attention to the new aircraft. Western thinking was focused on the vast Red Army with its thousands of tanks and Stalin's fanatical soldiers, rather than the Soviet air arm.

The USSR quickly demonstrated its capabilities to the West, including its impressive rate of production of modern fighters: 45 production MiG-15s flew over Moscow during the air parade on 1 May 1949. On 17 July at Tushino, 52 were seen. On 7 November 1949, no fewer than 90 took to the air over Red Square, and on 1 May 1950, 139 MiG-15s flew over Moscow. But the greatest

An Indonesian air force UTI-MiG-15. These aircraft were used for training of MiG-17 and MiG-19 pilots.

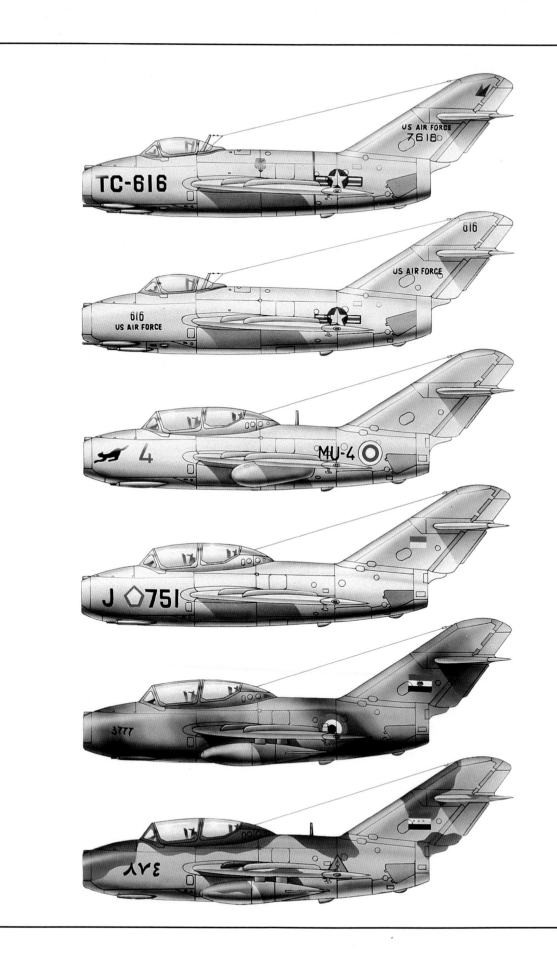

surprise to the West was the appearance of the MiG-15 in Korea, together with Soviet pilots.

Long after the Korean War, the MiG-15 received the NATO code name Falcon, which, because of its formidable sound, was quickly changed to Fagot. The UTI-MiG-15's code name was Midget.

In Korea, the MiG-15's superiority at high altitudes over the F-86 Sabre was an unpleasant surprise to pilots of the US Air Force (USAF) and to Western aircraft experts. The West undertook to obtain a MiG-15 for detailed investigation. These attempts produced a result in July 1951 when a MiG-15 was lifted from about 16ft (5m) of water off the Korean coast by ships of Britain's Royal Navy. That aircraft, produced at plant No. 1 in Kuibyshev (initial batch), was passed to the USAF for evaluation. [Editor's note: Available sources failed to confirm the retrieval of a MiG-15 by Royal Navy ships. Portions of a MiG-15 were recovered from a river mud flat by a US team transported behind the lines in an H-19 helicopter. The pieces were sent to Cornell Aero Lab, Buffalo, New York.]

The first MiG-15bis to reach the West was flown on 5 March 1953 (the day Stalin died) by Polish pilot Francizek Jarecki, who landed at the Danish island of Bornholm. At the same time, the UN allies were scattering leaflets over Korean territory offering a reward of $100,000 and political asylum to anyone who

Top to bottom: the MiG-15bis, manufacturer's number 2015337, that was flown to Kimpo Air Base near Seoul on 21 September 1953 by Korean pilot Ro Kim Suk. The aircraft was evaluated on Okinawa and at Wright-Patterson Air Force Base, Ohio, in 1954; the stolen MiG-15bis at Kadena Air Base, Okinawa; a Finnish air force UTI-MiG-15, one of four aircraft exported to Finland; an Indonesian air force UTI-MiG-15, exported in early 1960s, was used for training of Indonesian pilots for the MiG-17; an Egyptian air force UTI-MiG-15; and an Iraqi air force MiG-15 two-seater as seen in Prague, Czechoslovakia, in 1963, several days before delivery to the Middle East.

would deliver a MiG-15 to the UN side. No one responded to that alluring offer until two months after the end of the war, on 21 September 1953, when North Korean pilot Ro Kim Suk (who claimed not to have heard about the offer, but received the $100,000) flew his MiG-15 to Kimpo air base, near Seoul.

That aircraft (no. 2015337) underwent detailed evaluations and flight tests on Okinawa in 1953, where it was flown by Tom Collins and Charles Yeager, among others, and at Wright Field, Ohio, and Eglin Air Force Base, Florida, in 1954.

According to analysis by USAF specialists, there was nothing unusual in the MiG-15's structure. By Western estimation, it was a reliable combat aircraft but without special fuel, material, or other innovations. The weight of the aircraft was less than that of other swept-wing fighters, the MiG-15bis being 35 percent lighter than the F-86F and 47 percent lighter than the British Hunter. Western experts criticized the MiG's oversized inlet, low rate of fire, and absence of a radio rangefinder.

Apart from the war in Korea, the MiG-15 caused trouble for the West all over the world. During the Cold War, a dogfight with the MiG-15 promised nothing good for any Western aircraft. MiGs mercilessly shot down anything unlucky enough to be caught in the aiming reticle of their sights.

The first incident happened on 29 April 1952, when a MiG-15 attacked a French DC-4 over the Berlin corridor. On 11 May 1952, two Soviet MiG-15s intercepted a Martin PBM-5 Mariner flying boat over the Sea of Japan.

On 4 June 1952, an aircraft carrying the US Supreme Commissioner in Austria was forced to land at a Soviet air base. On 15 July 1952, an American RB-26 weather-reconnaissance aircraft was attacked over the Yellow Sea by a MiG-15. On 31 July 1952 in the same place, MiG-15s attacked another PBM-5 flying boat. On 8 October 1952, MiG-15bis forced a USAF C-47 flying over the Berlin corridor to land. On 18 November 1952 over the

Sea of Japan, a dogfight took place between four Soviet MiG-15s and three US Navy F9F Panthers. Two MiG-15s were shot down; one Panther was damaged.

On 15 March 1953, an American RB-50 reconnaissance aircraft was taken under fire by MiG-15 fighters to the east of Kamchatka. The next rendezvous was more tragic: on 29 July 1953, MiG-15s shot down another RB-50 over the Sea of Japan. On 22 January 1954, an American reconnaissance aircraft with 16 fighter escorts was attacked by eight MiG-15s over the Yellow Sea. One MiG-15 was shot down. On 7 November 1954, an RB-29 reconnaissance aircraft was shot down by a Soviet MiG-15 north of Hokkaido. On 5 February 1955, an American F-86 shot down a North Korean MiG-15 over the Sea of Japan. On 22 June 1955, a US Navy P2V Neptune was attacked by a MiG-15 and had to make an emergency landing on an island in the Bering Sea.

There were also emergency landings of Soviet aircraft in West Germany. The first information about Soviet aircraft often reached the West from Germany because VVS units in East Germany were first to convert to up-to-date aircraft.

MiG-15s of various models can be seen in collections in the West today. The MiG-15bis of North Korea's Lieutenant Ro Kim Suk is now in the USAF Museum. Several former Chinese J-2s were bought by private collectors. A Polish SB Lim-2 two-seater was imported to the United States and is used now by a private experimental organization. Another Polish Lim-2 appears in TV films representing enemies of the USA, including the film *Steal the Sky* in which it portrays an Iraqi fighter.

Next page
Top to bottom: a North Korean air force MiG-15bis; a later production series MiG-15bis equipped with OSP-48 system and RSIU-3 radio station of the Chinese air force; a Chinese air force MiG-15bis painted in standard camouflage scheme; a Czech-built UTI-MiG-15 (CS-102) of the East German air force; an East German air force MiG-15bis; and a Hungarian air force MiG-15bis.

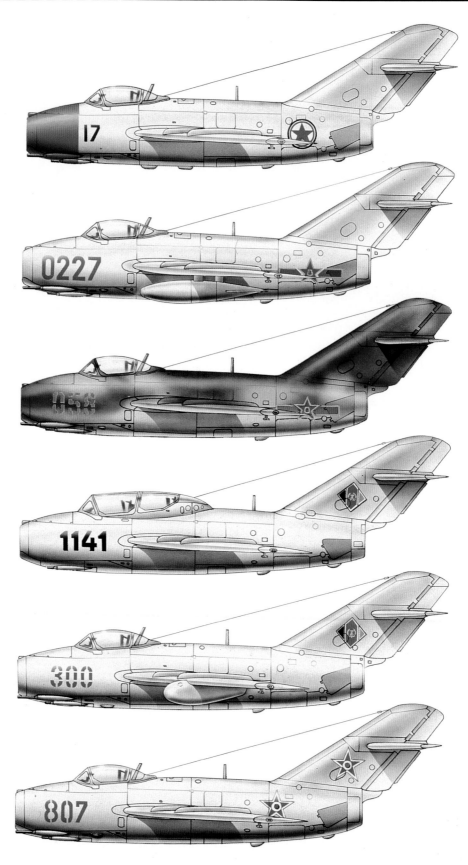

Chapter 4

Soviet Air Force MiG-15s in Combat in Korea

Military Operations in Korea

Participation of Soviet pilots and aircraft in postwar conflicts was a secret in the USSR until recently and little has been disclosed in the Soviet media, even today.

Much Russian thinking on the Korean War is based on Western sources. *Air Power As A Decisive Force in Korea* by J. Stewart, published in the USSR in 1959, may be the most objective source available to Russian readers on American operations in Korea and, to an extent, Soviet involvement. Other books were published in the West by historians and by American combat pilots.

Here, in contrast to the Western viewpoint, the authors attempt to describe those air battles of 40 years ago as they were seen by the Soviet side, including by actual participants—Soviet fighter pilots who flew MiG-15s in Korea and fought in hard battles against UN forces.

An air regiment from Kubinka was sent to China in February 1950—before the war began.The 29th FAR was transferred from Kubinka to China in August and September 1950, before MiGs entered the battle. The 151st FAD entered the war sometime later. These units flew the MiG-15s that American pilots first fought in November 1950.

Beside combat air units committed directly to battles, other Soviet air units in China provided air defense and trained Chinese and Korean pilots in jet aircraft. This group was under the command of S. Krasovsky who had much experience leading air units in the Great Patriotic War. The 64th Fighter Air Corps (FAC) formed directly for military operations in Korea included fighters, antiaircraft artillery, reconnaissance, and security units. The main function of the Corps was air defense of bridges and dams on the Yalu River.

The participation of Soviet pilots flying MiG-15 fighters in air battles in Korea can be divided into three stages.

The first stage lasted from November 1950 to April 1951, when the first Soviet combat units fought from Chinese air bases across the Yalu River from Korea and went into battle against the Americans, who held air superiority over North Korea. These forces succeeded in blunting the thrust of their adversary, but when the Americans introduced the F-86 Sabre, the period when F-51 Mustangs and F-80 Shooting Stars could be easily attacked came to an end.

American pilots first saw swept-wing fighters in Korean airspace on 1 November 1950—and contrary to what most Western historians have assumed, they were flown by Soviet pilots, not Chinese. F-51D Mustangs were attacked by MiG-15s near the Yalu River. The Americans knew nothing about this aircraft. Aircraft specialists had some information because of the MiG-15's appearance at Tushino in 1948, but American pilots were to pay a high price because the information had not been taken seriously. When it entered combat, the MiG-15 dashed toward F-80s and F-84 strike aircraft and shot them down.

Both sides operated under rigid restrictions, imposed by the UN on one side and on the other by the Soviet reluctance to expand the conflict. The USSR tried to conceal the participation of its pilots. UN pilots were prohibited from crossing the Yalu, and the Soviet MiG-15 pilots stayed behind an imaginary line drawn between Wonsan and Pyongyang in central North Korea. MiGs were also prohibited from operating over the sea. When Korean and Chinese pilots of the Joint Air Army started to fly combat in the summer of 1951, these prohibitions were not applied to them; they could fly where they wanted, but they suffered big losses when Soviet pilots were not available to protect them.

Soviet MiG pilots made effective use of the proximity of their home airfield to the Yalu River. This enabled them to save fuel during the first phases of air combat. As for the Sabres, they had already burned most of their fuel by the time the MiGs engaged them.

Though the Americans were officially prohibited from crossing the Yalu, they often did when they were in "hot pursuit" of a MiG. These attacks continued usually until the MiG touched its runway, when a kind of secret law took effect and the attack was broken off—but there were instances when Soviet MiGs were attacked on their airfields. Had the Americans bombed the MiG-15 bases, activity would have fallen sharply or dropped to zero, as shown eloquently by the way the Americans wiped out 34 airfields in North Korean territory.

The first battle between the F-86A and MiG-15 took place on 17 December 1950. Lt. Col. Bruce Hinton shot down the first MiG-15 in Korean airspace, firing some 1,500 .50cal (12.7mm) rounds.

The first large-scale jet battle took place on 22 December 1950. According to American sources, eight F-86As met 15 MiG-15s, and six MiG-15s were shot down. Through December, the Ameri-

Good photos of the MiG-15 during the Korean War are not easily available anywhere, even in Russia. Photographing these aircraft was strongly prohibited. This photo shows North Korean air force MiG-15s with noses painted red.

cans claimed eight MiG-15s, with the loss of only one Sabre in 16 skirmishes. We will consider the matter of losses by both sides below.

The Americans were not active against the MiGs from January to April 1951. A few F-86s were shifted to direct support of the ground troops that were engaged in heavy battles with the Chinese.

The first Soviet MiG-15 pilots did not have enough combat experience, and training of these pilots had to be improved. It was one thing to defeat F-51s and F-80s, and quite another to face F-86s. The commander of the 196th FAR, E. Pepelyaev, confirms that MiG pilots needed to hone their tactics.

Of course, the main goal of Soviet fighter aviation was to neutralize USAF bombers. From this point of view, avoiding combat with the F-86 can be justified.

The number of units involved in battles was limited by the availability of airfields. Only one, Antung, was ready for combat aircraft, while airfields at Manpo, Tapao, and elsewhere became available later. [Editor's note: These individual names may or may not match Western spellings of Korean locations. These names were translated directly from the Russian-language spellings on the Soviet source documents.] MiG-15s of the Ko-

rean-Chinese Joint Air Army were based at additional airfields from the summer of 1951. Attempts to use three airfields in North Korea failed because they were attacked systematically by UN air power.

The first stage of Soviet MiG-15 operations in Korea was completed when the first group of Soviet pilots left Antung and returned to the USSR as a unit in early 1951. This first stages had been very hard; witness the fact that Soviet pilots were honored with the title Hero of the Soviet Union, the top Soviet military award, when they destroyed three or four enemy aircraft. The Order of Lenin, or Order of the Red Banner, was given just for flying a certain number of combat missions. Because this first group gained combat experience through great sacrifice, pilots who replaced them had it easier. And the newer pilots were better trained, going to Korea as volunteers without illusions, prepared to confront an opponent with experience and a high-performance fighter.

The Soviets rotated whole units out of combat at once. Rotating air units (rather than individuals) through the Korean conflict had an inherent flaw. New pilots went into combat without experienced colleagues beside them. Newcomers "stepped on the same rake" (from a Russian joke about repeatedly making mistakes). Pilots who completed a tour of duty could pass along their experience only orally to newcomers. There was a decline of MiG activity after each turn-around of pilots, and one consequence was increased losses. The Americans, in contrast, rotated individuals, not squadrons. "Elders" coached newcomers as they gained experience. This rotation

scheme typifies the way Soviet leaders military and civil, approached any activity. If something did not succeed, shallow decisions, often not touching the cause of the problem, were usually taken. If F-86s won a battle with MiG-15s, Soviet pilots and commanders were blamed and then replaced.

The second stage was from April 1951 to January 1952. This stage was characterized by offensive operations by Chinese troops and intensified bombing by the Americans. The 324th Fighter Air Division (FAD) under top-scoring Great Patriotic War ace I. Kozhedub, three times Hero of the Soviet Union, and the 303rd FAD under G. Lobov (later, Kumanichkin) participated in battles from the communist side. The domination of American air power in Korea was reversed. The communist MiGs seized air superiority over the Yalu River area during that period. Each time American aircraft intruded into that zone, they suffered heavy losses. The American pilots nicknamed this zone MiG Alley.

The second group of pilots was selected more carefully than the first. The group was formed in the autumn of 1950 and started toward Manchuria in November. The 324th FAD consisted of the 196th FAR and the 176th Guard Fighter Air Regiment (GFAR), and was composed of volunteers who had accumulated high hours (by Soviet standards) in jet aircraft, particularly in the MiG-15. Many veterans of the Great Patriotic War were among them. The 303rd FAD under G. Lobov was formed simultaneously. The 324th FAD replaced the first batch of Soviet pilots in Korea and began combat duty in April 1951, flying from Antung.

Pepelyaev's 196th FAR had more success than other Soviet units. This regiment lost no aircraft or pilots but also destroyed no adversary aircraft in its first skirmishes. Less lucky, 176th GFAR lost three aircraft on its first combat mission. Pepelyaev coached his pilots harshly, so the Russian motto "hard in study, easy in battle" was true for them.

The arrival of the 304th FAD, consisting of three fighter air regiments, occurred in June 1951. Simultaneously, the airfield at Manpo was made ready for combat operations. Also in June, the Americans identified new combat units of MiG-15s with a new paint scheme featuring red noses and tail fins. These were aircraft of the 303rd FAD.

In time, Soviet fighters succeeded in countering daytime activity by B-29 bombers. The B-29s switched to night raids after 30 October 1951, or Black Tuesday, when the Americans lost twelve B-29s and four F-84 Thunderjets, according to Soviet sources. [Editor's note: American records show that three B-29s were lost, four more were damaged and forced to divert, and only one returned to its home base. While both sides always exaggerate aerial victory claims in warfare, loss records are usually accurate. Actual American losses were three B-29s and one F-84.] According to Soviet sources no Soviet-flown MiG-15s were destroyed by B-29 gunners. [F-86s claimed two MiG-15s but were prevented from assisting a B-29 force escorted only by inadequate F-84 Thunderjets. The F-84s claimed one MiG, suffered one loss, and were helpless to prevent the MiGs from mauling the bombers. B-29 gunners claimed three MiGs.] The poor efficiency of B-29's defensive weaponry against the MiG-15 was evident in these battles. There was damage, but no MiG-15s were shot down.

The deliveries of new MiG-15bis with better performance than basic MiG-15, to Korea had begun in the summer of 1951. Simultaneously, the USAF began to introduce a new version of the Sabre, the F-86E with an all-flying tail. MiGs fought American fighters-bombers in the daytime, restricting to a great extent their capacity to directly support ground troops. The MiG-15 was chosen for night missions against the B-29 in December 1951 because the La-11, the primary aircraft of the Night Fighter Regiments, was too slow to counter the B-29.

Pilots of the 324th FAD made a mortal strike against No. 77 Squadron of the Royal Australian Air Force, flying Meteor Mk.VIII fighters. The Soviet MiGs claim to have destroyed many of the Australian aircraft during the second stage of Soviet involvement.

According to the Soviet sources, the 324th FAD destroyed 207 enemy aircraft, including 104 shot down by the 196th FAR and 103 by the 176th GFAR, by February 1952. The 303rd FAD, operating simultaneously with the 324th, destroyed 303 UN aircraft. According to the Soviets, the total number of UN aircraft shot down by the Soviet pilots reached 510 in less than a year of a conflict. [Editor's note: Loss records of UN air forces indi-

To Catch a Sabre

The way the Americans got a MiG-15 is covered elsewhere in this narrative. Now it is time to reveal how the USSR got an F-86A.

Offering a reward, as the UN side did, was not the solution. Nobody was going to waste money trying to corrupt American pilots. The Soviet government seemed to guess that no one with common sense would fly toward the Soviet territory. What F-86 pilot would want to spend the rest of his days in Siberia or to get a bullet into his nape? So the leadership of the aviation units operating in Korea were ordered to capture a Sabre by any means.

When the first attempts to do it failed, because the Americans were destroying all their F-86s shot down, a special group of test pilots of GK NII VVS with Lt. Gen. A. Blagoveschensky at the head was sent to a region of military operations. This group arrived in Antung in April 1951 and began to cooperate with the 196th FAR. The group had the purpose of collecting information about new American combat aircraft. This information was necessary for the designing of the new Soviet I-350, I-360, and La-190 fighters.

Pilots of the Blagoveschensky group made attempts to force Sabres to land at their airfield, but this ended quite sadly. One MiG-15 was shot down during the first attempt, and two others were seriously damaged. The attempt was repeated eight days later, after the tactics of the enemy and the experience of pilots of the 196th FAR were analyzed. Again, there was a failure. Test pilot Lt. Col. Dzubenko damaged his MiG in an attempt to force down a Sabre. He perished while landing when his damaged MiG-15 turned over on the runway. Later, the Blagoveschensky group returned to the USSR, having lost one more pilot. Valuable facts on American combat aircraft were collected. Some of the pilots of this group remained fighting in Korea and many became aces.

Efforts to snare a Sabre succeeded at last: Lt. Col. E. Pepelyaev, commander of the 196th FAR, shot down an F-86A in the autumn of 1951, the F-86A made an emergency landing on a sand bank in the coastal region, and American aircraft failed to destroy it from the air (for more details see Pepelyaev's account in chapter 7). The captured F-86A was delivered to An-

tung and moved onward to Moscow in two days.

In Moscow, the Sabre was examined by the OKBs of the Ministry of Aviation Industry and also in ministries adjacent to it. The results were used to develop and improve Soviet aircraft systems.

In particular, the Mikoyan OKB examined carefully the F-86A control system on a special stand. The F-86 control system was reverse engineered and underwent tests at the plant. An in-depth test and research program was held later to reveal numerous nuances of US technology.

Elements of the Sabre's air-conditioning system were mounted in a MiG-17 cockpit and were tested at altitudes up to 39,360ft (12,000km). The gun-sight radar was studied in detail. Results of these investigations accelerated designing the first Soviet ranging radars of the SRD series. Research into electric equipment, in particular, yielded valuable material for improvement of Soviet aircraft AC and DC converters. The majority of OKBs got interesting and valuable data from studying the Sabre.

Stalin was determined to copy Sabre technology, production methods, and materials and gave the project high priority. A group of specialists under the leadership of designer Kondratyev began to execute the order of "People's Father" at the former P. Sukhoi OKB facilities (the OKB had been closed since 1949 and was restored only in 1953). The American technologies and new aluminium alloys were copied. And study of the Sabre gave other positive results. In 1953 this group became a part of the Sukhoi OKB and began working on new jet aircraft designs. Designers, technologists, and workers adopted the elements of the American technical culture of production and assembling. As a result, the general technical level of the re-formed Sukhoi OKB became higher than that of the other Soviet OKBs.

Just as the B-29 helped to develop the aviation industry in the USSR, similarly the captured F-86A Sabre served briefly but gave good service to Soviet supersonic aviation of the first generation in the early 1950s. According to the best information available, the F-86 was never flown in the USSR, and its ultimate fate is unknown.

Chinese "volunteers" suffered high attrition in manpower and materiel because of their inexperience and chronically malnourished condition. Skilled American pilots won many air battles flying against the Chinese.

cate that the allies lost about 40 aircraft, not 510, during the first year of the MiG-15's involvement.]

Soviet losses totaled 22 aircraft of the 324th FAD and almost 30 aircraft of the 303rd FAD, or a total of about 50 MiG-15s. Thus, the ratio was 10:1 to the benefit of the MiG-15 with Soviet pilots during this period, if we count all UN aircraft shot down and not just F-86s.

According the data of Gen. G. Lobov, Soviet pilots brought down over 1,300 adversary aircraft in Korean airspace, while Soviet losses totaled 345 MiG-15s. American sources list 971 USAF aircraft lost in the Korean War to all causes, including 58 Sabres in air-to-air combat. The losses include aircraft shot down by enemy fighters, destroyed by antiaircraft artillery, as well as noncombat losses. The Americans claim 792 MiG-15s brought down. While Soviet sources acknowledge that 345 Soviet MiGs were shot down, loss records for the Korean-Chinese Joint Air Army remain unavailable. The claim of 792 MiGs destroyed is evidently exaggerated because some of these MiG-15s, seemingly shot down on Sabre gun-camera film, actually landed at their airfields with damage. Soviet pilots had a stricter system of counting aerial victories: evidence from military men on the ground or from civil authorities, as well as photo film and a report by the pilot and his mates was re-quired. If a UN aircraft downed by MiGs fell in territory where this confirmation was impossible, the kill often was not credited. Even so, aerial victories claimed by both sides seem equally inflated, in the view of the authors. To quote E. Pepelyaev, "Not everything that was scored was actually shot down!"

Measuring losses on both sides is an equally tricky thing and both sides downplayed losses. The Americans claim that they lost 58 Sabres in air battles. But a single squadron of the 196th FAR counted 28 F-86s shot down. This was one of many Russian squadrons flying combat missions, and the North Korean and Chinese pilots were sure to have claimed many Sabres.

The third stage of Soviet involvement ran from the beginning of 1952 until the end of the Korean war. The Americans began night B-29 operations, intensified day strikes by fighter-bombers, and introduced advanced versions of the Sabre. Chinese MiG-15 pilots played an increased role, often flying in big fighter formations, but they sustained high losses because of poor combat skills. Still, although with flaws, MiG forces maintained an effective defense, and UN air power could not restore the supremacy it had enjoyed earlier.

Combat units from Soviet Air Defense Aviation (Aviatsiya PVO) began to relieve the second group of Soviet pilots in January 1952. The third period of participation of MiGs in battles in Korea had begun. The 97th FAD of the PVO, officially deemed ready for battle, but in fact not ready at all, replaced the 324th. Losses grew.

The Americans initiated powerful raids on North Korean communication and other targets of DPRK, engaging in air combat with Soviet MiGs even over China. The 97th FAD turned out to be well prepared only on paper.

Additional Soviet fighter units reached Korea near the end of the war but their level of combat readiness, too, was low. Accordingly, they scored fewer kills of UN aircraft and sustained higher losses.

UN fighters-bombers, flying daytime strikes, suddenly became the main threat to Soviet pilots. The composition of USAF fighter-bomber units changed dramatically. F-86Fs took over the fighter bomber role, replacing the F-80. Now night B-29 raids were escorted by F-94B and F3D-2 Skyknights so that nocturnal combat was filled with drama for both sides. The Soviet fleet also changed, re-equipping with late MiG-15bis.

As a night interceptor, the MiG-15, lacking radar, was guided to the combat area by a GCI (ground control intercept) station and then sought visual contact with the target with the help of a searchlight. Pilots took advantage of moonlight or the glow of a jet exhaust, if any.

When B-29s began night raids on targets in North Korea, the 351st FAR of night fighters, flying the La-11, was assigned to counter them. Attempts by the La-11 to intercept B-29s at night rarely succeeded. The best night pilot of the 64th FAC, A. Karelin, shot down only one B-29 flying the La-11. In December 1951 the Soviets urgently decided to employ the MiG-15bis for part of the night commitment after Karelin failed to intercept another B-29 even though the bomber was perfectly illuminated by searchlights.

One of the 351st FAR's squadrons converted to the MiG-15bis in February 1952 (the other retaining the La-11). Pilots of the 97th FAD with night experience began to fly nocturnal missions.

A. Karelin scored the first MiG night victory, bringing down his second B-29 (his first in a MiG-15) at the end of spring. As USAF night raids continued to increase, two more squadrons of MiG-15bis for night operations were formed.

In the Korean night, MiG-15s faced not only B-29s but F-94Bs and F3D-2s. Even with no radar, MiG-15s sometimes were guided by GCI so precisely that they accidentally rammed the American aircraft. I. Kovalev collided with an F-94B at 32,800ft (10,000m) in the darkness on 7

November 1952. Kovalev struck the other aircraft with the belly of his MiG-15, and both aircraft burst into flames. Their pilots ejected safely. [Editor's note: American sources do not confirm this account, which also does not speak to the fate of the F-94B radar operator.]

Karelin brought down his fourth B-29 in autumn of 1952. Again, the unexpected happened. Following GCI guidance to the target, Karelin collided with the B-29, slapping his MiG's gun mount against the bomber's tail gun. The B-29 tail gunner started firing wildly, unable to see the MiG. Having identified the B-29 by the muzzle flash from its tail gun, Karelin fired a salvo from all his guns and brought the bomber down.

Karelin scored his fifth and last night kill, a B-29, in February 1953. This time, the gunner of the B-29 had time to hit Karelin's MiG-15. Its fuel pipeline was damaged causing the engine to shut down, but Karelin succeeded in gliding to a landing. There were 117 holes in his MiG, including nine in the cockpit.

RB-29s that flew post-strike reconnaissance missions appeared in Antung's airspace after a massive raid on the Supung dam and power station on 12 January 1953. Y. Khabiev from the 535th FAR (which also flew night missions) was sent to intercept one. Khabiev attacked the RB-29 and set it aflame with his first shot. The RB-29 began to descend after the second attack, and its crew began to bail out. Eleven of 14 crewmen escaped safely. Among them were Col. Knox Arnold, Jr., and Maj. William Horl Bowmer, commander of the USAF 91st Strategic Reconnaissance Squadron. This RB-29 (serial no. 44-62217) took off from Japan and was brought down in Chinese airspace. [Editor's note: American sources do not confirm the facts in this account.]

Y. Dobrovichan shot down two B-29s in one night combat in January 1953 and was awarded the Order of Lenin.

According to the Soviet nonofficial sources, MiG-15s shot down or heavily damaged 18 B-29s and three F-94Bs in night combat up to March 1953. But this data must be questioned.

Soviet Tactics

To combat the F-86, the MiG-15 fought in a basic unit of two aircraft, or pair. The two members of a pair never separated from each other, since a single pilot alone would face increased danger

from the enemy. Early in Korean fighting, MiG-15s operated in groups of eight (or, in Soviet terminology, two flights, since the Russians view a flight as two pairs). This was deemed a suitable size for supportive interaction in air combat.

But in 1951, Soviet MiG-15 pilots began to fly at high altitudes in groups of six rather than eight. A group of six offered flexibility and safety for the whole group.

A squadron of MiGs on combat duty was considered as a shift. The first shift, being in the squadron house, traversed into the third in 2hr, the second into the first, the third into the second. The first shift received "Readiness No.1" by the signal from the command tower.

After takeoff, a flight of MiG-15s often loitered above the objective they were defending, such as the electrical power stations and bridges on the Yalu River. These flights were arranged in two layers. GCI operators informed the MiG pilots about the enemy's approach. The upper layer of MiGs moved against the enemy with the advantage of altitude and speed, to engage on favorable terms. The F-86 Sabres were there to prevent the MiGs from attacking Allied fighter-bombers and other aircraft.

The GCI alert system was based on a scheme proven in the Great Patriotic War. While on the ground waiting to be scrambled on a GCI intercept, pilots sat in their cockpits as little as possible to

Soviet MiG-15s participated in the Korean War with rudders and fuselage noses painted in red.

Soviet ace Evgeny Pepelyaev shot down nineteen United Nations aircraft in Korea.

E. Belyaev, commander of the Excellent Flight, defines a mission to his pilots.

A rare photo from the Korean War period. This group of Soviet pilots participated in combat operations against American and United Nations aircraft. The commander of the regiment, Evgeny Pepelyaev, is fourth from left in the lower row.

conserve their strength in the hot, wet climate. The main GCI station, with information from air-defense radars, monitored the threat and scrambled MiG-15s.

Two combat sorties per day was the average for MiG-15 pilots during the war in Korea. Differing from MiG-15 with its purpose of defence, the Sabres were free to choose the time and methods of aerial attacks, so the initiative belonged to them. [Editor's note: It is interesting to note that American Sabre pilots felt that the MiG-15 pilots held the initiative because they operated close to their airfields, could remain behind the Yalu if they chose to, and could begin a fight with the advantage of higher altitude.] After a fight, results were analyzed in preparation for the next sortie or shift. Of great importance was analysis of the combat performance of the enemy, who often changed tactics. After hard combat, the Americans had relaxed periods during which they corrected errors and worked out new tactics.

In the Korean War, a Soviet squadron was divided into three groups for different tactics and purposes: attack, cover (known in American terms as CAP, or combat air patrol), and reserve. The attack group included no less than one flight and was intended to destroy the enemy's main force. The goal of the cover group was to defend the attack group and to reinforce it. The reserve (one or two pairs) supported these groups and also parried attacks by any enemy fighters that tried to join the fight. If not needed, the reserve was not committed to battle.

Cover and attack groups were usually arranged one above the other. Separation equalled the vertical distance that the aircraft routinely needed during a combat turn. This facilitated coordination of the group in combat. In this case, one pair was responsible to function as the reserve, supporting the cover and attack groups. Groups of six offered better flexibility.

Pilots who were out front surveyed the forward hemisphere, while those in the rear visually covered the rear hemisphere. The searching pair, upon detecting the enemy, was the first to begin the attack and the remaining MiGs provided cover or added to the combat effort.

These tactics sharply increased the role of a pair of fighters. A pair usually comprised pilots with equal tactical skills, able to pass to each other the functions of "shield" and "sword" in combat. Full psychological compatibility, and a shared understanding of the logic of the combat made a pair of MiG-15 pilots formidable in combat.

The most widely used tactic of the MiG-15 in Korea was to "hit and run." After receipt of information from GCI, a head-on approach was typically the beginning of an engagement. The MiG-15 usually held the initial advantage of higher altitude. This advantage was used by pairs of MiG pilots who swooped down at high speed, one after the other. If the enemy broke formation and began defensive maneuvers during the attack of the first pair, the second pair changed direction and chose the most vulnerable target. After attacking, MiGs immediately climbed away using the speed gained during the descent. They did not enter into prolonged combat, but repeated the original tactic whenever possible. This method depended on good timing and, when well-executed, made it difficult for the enemy to begin offensive action since the Sabre did not have enough thrust to climb with the MiGs.

A first attack employing a half roll that ended in a gun turn often brought an immediate end to the fight. A form of this maneuver, called "hump to the sun," was an improvement on the "hit and run." This attack began from the sun side and ended with egress toward the sun. Its success depended upon the excellent climbing speed of the MiG-15.

The tactic called "roundabout" was used during point defense of ground targets. Two pairs of MiG-15s formed a circle and the pilots covered each other. There were two or three such circles, and the pairs were arranged in echelon by altitude. The upper pair moved toward the enemy. Sabres usually attacked the lower echelon. Then, a hit-and-run attack descended on them from above. The MiG-15, coming out of the attack, then went into a new circle. The principle of coordination between groups of fighters had to be strictly observed when using this method.

A "pincers" tactic was sometimes used. Two flights of MiG-15s headed south at slightly diverging routes at 32,800ft (10,000m). The flights were separated beyond visible limits, so GCI coordinated its operations. Before meeting the enemy, the MiGs descended to 14,500–19,400ft (4,500–6,000m) altitude

Soviet pilots, veterans of the Korean War, during one of their reunions.

The MiG-15bis of Korean Sr. Lt. Ro Kum Suk (number 2057) shortly after defection to South Korea on 21 September 1953, probably in Okinawa. USAF via Steve Zaloga

Number 2057 after transfer to Wright-Patterson Air Force Base in 1953. The MiG is painted in revised Soviet/North Korean Air Force markings. USAF via Steve Zaloga

Rear view of 2057 after it had been repainted in USAF markings. USAF via Steve Zaloga

Heroes of the Soviet Union

During the war in Korea 22 Soviet pilots gained the title of the Hero of the Soviet Union. Herein is the list of them by date that the award was given:

Stepan Bakhaev, major, Deputy Squadron Leader—166 combat missions flown/11 aircraft shot down

Arkady Boitsov, Captain, Deputy Squadron Leader—no data

Nikolay Dokaschenko, Captain, Flight Commander, —148/11

Grigory Ges', Captain, Squadron Leader—120/9

Anatolay Karelin, Major, Deputy Commander of the Fighter Air Regiment—50/5

Sergey Kramenko, Captain, Deputy Squadron Leader—149/13

Georgy Lobov, Major General, Commander of the 64th Fighter Air Corps—15/4(he gained his rank during World War II, where he flew 356 combat missions and shot down 19 aircraft personally and 8 in group combats)

Mikhail Mikhin, Captain, Deputy Squadron Leader—no data available on missions flown, but he scored 11 victories

Stepan Nazarenko, Major, Deputy Squadron Leader—no data

Boris Obraztsov, 1st Lieutenant—no data

Dmitry Os'kin, Major, Commander of the Fighter Air Regiment—150/15

Grigory Okhai, Captain, Deputy Commander of the Fighter Air Regiment—122/11

Evgeny Pepelyaev, Colonel, Commander of the Fighter Air Regiment—108/23

Mikhail Ponomarev, Captain, Squadron Leader—140/14

Grigory Pulov, Lieutenant Colonel, Commander of the Fighter Air Regiment—120/8

Dmitry Samoilov, 1st Lieutenant—161/10

Alexander Smorchkov, Lieutenant Colonel, Deputy Commander of the Air Fighter Regiment—191/15

Evgeny Stel'makh, 1st Lieutenant—15/1(award honored posthumously for personal heroism)

Serafim Subbotin, Captain, Navigator of the Fighter Air Regiment—no data concerning missions but he scored 15 victories

Nikolay Sutyagin, Captain, Deputy Squadron Leader—150/21

Fedor Shebanov, 1st Lieutenant—150/6

Lev Schukin, Captain, Flight Commander—212/15

and turned to the north, designing the turn to meet each other. On the return route, the flight searched for USAF fighter-bombers and small groups of Sabres heading back to their bases. A third flight (sometimes a pair) of MiG-15s penetrated the space created by this pincer at a time calculated to facilitate a kill of the enemy aircraft. In some cases, this flight or pair had the added purpose of covering MiGs returning from a mission with limited fuel.

The tactic known as "distraction" was complicated and MiG pilots employed it only after gaining enough combat experience. The intention was to lure the patrolling Sabres from their zones while directing the MiG-15s toward the south to engage USAF attack aircraft. GCI ordered entry of the group of fighters into released airspace. The "distraction" group was there to lure the Sabres away, but was not excluded from engaging the F-86s for the larger goal of air defense.

The tactic called "snare" was an active method that involved sending MiGs out as bait. The squadron of MiGs formed a "ladder," descending toward the enemy in pairs, flights, or sixes. The lower echelon consisted of separate pairs that attracted the patrolling Sabres. But the MiGs from this bait group didn't accept combat and got away by climbing. The Sabres pursuing the bait now faced attack from above on disadvantageous terms.

The tactic of "jaws" was similar to the snare. If the Sabres tried to climb after the bait MiGs, the main group of MiGs formed a ladder in two echelons, one above another, and the Sabres faced attack by the lower echelon.

The tactic "hit from underneath" was used against fighters and fighter-bombers flying at low altitude. Pairs of MiG-15s, composed of the most skilled pilots, flew to the area of combat at extremely low altitude and destroyed the detected enemy aircraft. Exploiting the mountainous terrain, they disengaged quickly.

Planning of possible situations and of each tactic depended on the actual combat situation. Fighting the F-86 Sabre with these tactics demanded careful planning. MiG-15 pilots took off, already prepared to use a certain tactic but knowing that the situation could change quickly.

The war ended in armistice on 27 July 1953, but Soviet pilots and MiG-15s moved to North Korea, where they remained until 1954.

During the war, 22 Soviet pilots earned the Hero of the Soviet Union award. One, S. Bakhaev, claimed 11 aerial victories. A. Karelin was honored for his night-fighting achievements. E. Pepelyaev, too, received the honor. Oddly, many pilots who scored up to ten aerial victories did not gain this title.

Pepelyaev had the best combat ratio, or number of victories per one combat mission flown, 0.21. He shot down one adversary enemy aircraft for each four missions. It took N. Sutyagin six missions to bring down one aircraft.

Capt. J. D. McConnell, highest-scoring American ace of the Korean War, had 16 victories in 106 combat missions.

Chapter 5

Korean War Stories of Soviet MiG-15 Pilots

Recent changes in the former Soviet Union revealed details about historical events hidden until recently under wraps of security. Only now can we better assess the capabilities of the MiG-15 in the Korean War and the combat actions in Korea. Below are reminiscence of leading Soviet fighter pilots who flew the MiGs in combat.

Lt. Gen. Georgy Lobov

During the Korean war Georgy Lobov, then already a lieutenant general, was first commander of the 303rd FAD (Fighter Air Division) and later of the 64th FAC (Fighter Air Corps). He served in Korea from early 1951 to the end of 1952. Lobov flew 15 combat missions and shot down four enemy aircraft.

Born in 1915, Lobov took part in the war against Finland in 1939–1940. During the Great Patriotic War he flew 346 sorties in which he shot down 19 German aircraft in solo flight and eight in formation missions. He was wounded in combat twice, and ended the war as commander of a fighter division. Lobov became a major general in 1947 taking the post of commander of a PVO fighter division.

The USAF established air superiority in the first weeks of the war. Being small and flying only piston-engine aircraft, the North Korean air force fought hard but was defeated. Chinese fighter aviation was only then converting to jet aircraft and not ready for combat operations.

I was sent to command the 303rd FAD, and later the Soviet fighter group, the 64th FAC.

USAF planning attached importance to actions against the peaceful population of North Korea, as well as to testing new weapons in a real combat environment. Thus, a plan for destroying water storage dams was found among the wreck of a B-26 bomber that had been shot down at night by ack-ack fire. This plan was called Operation Strangle and its aim was the destruction of irrigation installations and deprivation of the North Korean population of their main food product, rice. [Editor's note: Operation Strangle was a combined arms, air-ground effort against the Chinese army and was directed neither toward hydroelectric dams (which were attacked at a later date) nor the civilian population.]

With a group of commanders of fighter units based in the USSR's Primorsky territory, I visited China and North Korea to study the situation after the war broke out. The next day, after a massive onslaught by 79 B-29 bombers on the town of Sinuiju, we saw the results of the raid. There were no targets of any military importance in the town. Instead, an airfield and crossings over the Yalu River were in the vicinity, but not a single bomb had been dropped on them. The purpose of the attack was quite clear, the killing of the civilian population of the town and of numerous refugees from the South, as well as imposing terror on the North Korean population to break its will to fight.

Involuntarily, Dresden of 1945 came to mind, as well as other massive bomber raids by British and American aircraft, in which hundreds of thousands of civil inhabitants were killed. Not a single bomb fell on Klotze airfield in the outskirts of Dresden, where a Luftwaffe pilot school was situated.

In the Korean conflict, all Soviet fighter aviation and antiaircraft artillery units were incorporated into the 64th Separate Fighter Air Corps. In 1952 at the time of my command, this included three air divisions, two antiaircraft artillery divisions (85mm antiaircraft cannons, 57mm automatic guns), radio engineering units (radars, type P-3, detection and gun laying stations), an aircraft maintenance division, and three separate regiments: a night fighter regiment (flying the La-11 and MiG-15), a naval air regiment, and a searchlight regiment (to support fighter-interceptor operations at night and to create a "light" field in the Yalu crossing area and at the approaches to the river), two hospitals, and other support and logistics units.

In 1952, the 64th FAC numbered 26,000 men, a figure that did not change until war's end. We were far short of staffing requirements. Only half of the divisions had three regiments each, the rest only two. Only 32 pilots were assigned to each unit.

We faced difficulties caused by our manning system at that time. During the Great Patriotic War, combat air units were reinforced with trained pilot replacements just before air battles or during them. The Americans did this in Korea.

People were replaced in the 64th FAC by relieving an entire division at a time. Arriving replacements had only a vague idea of combat tactics. This caused newly arrived units to lose many rookie pilots. Besides, participation by the VVS in this war was secret and was concealed from our own citizens (though it was not a secret for the rest of the world). Experience gained at the expense of our pilots' lives was studied by VVS and by PVO officers, but was kept was strictly confidential.

In addition, in many air units, flight safety rather than battle training enjoyed high priority. Air commanders of all ranks were forced to simplify training. For example, training flights were made in close combat formations and, as a rule, with external tanks that limited maneuverability. Mock air battles during training were waged against targets that were not maneuvering or mounting any opposition. We addressed higher authorities criticizing this faulty system of training and replacing pilots. But all remained as it was. It was simpler to move entire divisions with a stroke of the pen, rather than to train every regiment, every pilot, for coming battles.

Soviet air units were put into combat sequentially. The number of fighters increased as the air situation became more complicated. However, this number never neared the fantastic totals claimed by the American side. The total strength of our aircraft did not exceed the strength of the Americans' 4th and 51st Fighter Wings of the US 5th Air Force. And, if all the fighters, fighter-bombers, and bombers of the USAF, Navy, and Marines and of US allies are counted, we were outnumbered eight or ten to one. [Editor's note: Lobov's figures do not count the Chinese and North Korean fighter units.]

We fought alone against Allied air power which held the initiative and had numerous aircraft capable of combat in day and night and in adverse weather. The enemy had F-94B all-weather radar-equipped fighter-interceptors, the F-95B Starfire, and great numbers of reconnaissance and electronic countermeasures aircraft. The Americans had a well-equipped airfield network. [Editor's note: The Americans regarded South Korea airfields as congested and primitive. Typically for pilots on both sides, Lobov does not remember all aircraft types accurately. The Americans had no plane called the F-95B Starfire.]

Since we were the defensive side, we were obliged to keep Soviet pilots on alert in their cockpits awaiting takeoff clearance and guidance to their targets. This was torture in humid and hot conditions. The initiative was in the hands of the Americans, who flew missions based on plans drawn up in advance and did not face these difficulties. We had to adapt our actions to theirs. They began the game and we ended it. Furthermore, the enemy possessed a large reserve of pilots that we lacked. And USAF fighter pilots withstood acceleration in battle better, as they wore special anti-G suits. Our PPK-1 anti-G suits were put into service only when the Korean war was over.

We faced many difficulties due to the order forbidding combat over the sea and pursuing enemy aircraft south of the Pyongyang–Wonsan line. The Americans made the best use of this circumstance. They carried out battles mainly near the sea coast. When they found themselves at a disadvantage, they quickly went toward the sea and from there, after choosing a convenient moment and taking advantageous position, they could engage in combat again or withdraw without hindrance. Our adversary was restricted, however, by the Chinese border. In spite of all this, our pilots went deep into the south, and the Americans crossed the Yalu, attacking our aircraft during their takeoffs and landings.

The mountainous terrain limited the capabilities of ground-based radar to detect and track aircraft. (The P-3 type radar with a detection range of 70–100mi (110–160km), which went into service in 1945, was used in Korea.) Therefore, the Soviet Air Command had to make decisions in a difficult environment and in the shortest time possible. Due to this, target interception was not always effected in time, in optimum formation, or at an effective altitude. Besides, our forward-based aviation suffered an acute shortage of airfields. At first, we had only Antung. Then, by July 1951, Manpo was put into operation. And in 1952, Tapao airfield was placed into service. This congestion reduced the effectiveness of Soviet fighters. But we were able to take off suddenly and place into the air large fighter forces from a small number of airfields, which was difficult to do quickly and, at times, simply impossible. (Though there were 34 North Korean airfields south of the Yalu, all them were thoroughly bombed by American aircraft at the slightest evidence of readiness for MiGs.)

Committing the Soviet MiG-15 jet aircraft and then the MiG-15bis to combat affected the general air situation in Korea immediately. Our first engagements against B-29s showed the effectiveness of the 23mm and 37mm guns in the MiGs. Security of the B-29s could not be assured even by numerous American fighter escorts.

Of course, the Soviet fighter cannons did not guarantee success in combat. The B-29s possessed heavy defensive armament and were invariably escorted by fighters. A victory was determined by proper tactics for the situation, good organization and efficient control of air combat, and the high personal skill of our pilots.

There are many examples proving this.

On 12 April 1951, a force of 48 B-29s escorted by dozens of fighters mounted a raid on the railway bridge across the Yalu, near Antung. They were met by 36 Soviet MiG-15s. Nine B-29s were shot down in the battle. All the MiG-15s returned to Antung airfield. The American version of this battle is as follows: the B-29s were attacked by 72–84 MiG-15s. Three B-29s were shot down. Seven were damaged. Nine to 15 MiGs were shot down and four MiGs were damaged by B-29s' defensive fire. [Editor's note: Lobov gives both a Soviet view and his version of the American view on what happened that day, when B-29s dropped 2,000lb (907kg) bombs on the Sinuiju bridge. In fact, American records indicate "bitter aerial opposition" by MiGs but no losses and no claims of aerial victories on that date.]

Especially heavy losses were suffered by the USAF in the air battle on 30 October the same year. This day went down in the history of the Korean War as Black Tuesday.

The term "air battle" truly applies here since 270 aircraft were engaged in the skirmish at a time and because of its consequences. A force of 21 B-29s covered by 200 fighters of various types was used in the raid. The aim of the raid was Namsi airfield in North Korea.

Black Tuesday was caused in part by errors by the USAF in planning the raid. The bombers and F-84 escort fighters were at different altitudes, and we knew from seeing the fighters on radar whom they were escorting and where they were going.

We possessed a total of 56 MiG-15s (of the 324th and 303rd FADs) at Antung and Manpo airfields. Twelve aircraft were kept in reserve to be used if the enemy crossed the river and 44 MiGs were put into the fight.

Considering the delay by the F-86 covering party and the inadequate escort arrangement, we did not earmark any special groups for fighting the Sabres. All of our MiG-15s were assigned to hit the B-29s. We also chose not to fly in large formations but in pairs, leaving each to its own resources. Our efforts were determined only by the location of the B-29s. This enabled each pair of MiGs to act with initiative and to maneuver freely.

We intercepted the enemy on approach to Namsi. While the F-86s searched for us near the Yalu, the fate of the battle and the lot of the B-29s were decided. Twenty-two pairs of MiG-15s swiftly dived through the F-84 escort fighters' formation at a speed of about 620mph (1,000km/h) and attacked the bombers. One hundred and thirty-two rapid-firing cannons were throwing fire into the enemy aircraft. The F-84s, being themselves under the threat of destruction, broke off and withdrew toward the sea. Four F-84s were shot down. [Editor's note: American loss records show that one F-84 and three B-29s were shot down that day.]

The first attack of the MiGs proved a success, the aim achieved. Before they could bomb their target, the B-29s were burning, falling, and turning away toward the sea.

Since the B-29's route was only 12–18mi (20–30km) from the coast, beyond which we were forbidden to fly, some bombers escaped. According to evidence from a B-29 navigator captured later, there were killed or wounded crewmen aboard all of the B-29s that escaped the MiG attacks. Not a single bomb fell on Namsi airfield.

Actually, neither in that air battle nor in any other, absurd as it sounds, did we suffer a single MiG loss from the defensive fire of the B-29s. Fights against B-29s favored our MiG-15s for a number of reasons. Our cannons had a much greater damage capacity than the B-29's .50cal (12.7mm) machine guns. Besides, B-29s demonstrated poor survivability. The computing devices and the gun mounts themselves did not provide for aiming at, and effectively firing on, fighters attacking at a high closing rate. An attack itself lasted only 3–4sec. [Editor's note: The Tupolev OKB, when reverse engineering the B-29, copied almost everything without any changes, except that defensive armament that was changed to 20mm cannons.]

The results of the Black Tuesday were troubling to USAF officials. Not a single American aircraft appeared in the area where Soviet MiGs operated for three days. About a month later, sixteen of our fighters intercepted three B-29s covered by dozens of F-86s at the approaches to the crossings at Anju. All the bombers were shot down. We did not suffer any losses. [Editor's note: After Black Tuesday, when three B-29s were lost, the B-29 strikes shifted to the nocturnal hours. According to American loss records, never again were three B-29s shot down in a single day.]

There arose the question of further production of piston-engine heavy bombers such as the B-50 and B-36. A speeded-up transition to jet bombers started. But because of conservative thinking by USAF leaders, I believe the result would have been no different if the B-47 had been in the B-29's place.

The transition by all of the B-29s to night missions resulted in an immediate reaction from our side. We quickly re-equipped night fighter units from piston-engine La-11s to the MiG-15bis which, unlike the American F-94B, lacked airborne radar.

After several B-29s were shot down at night, the Americans took measures to protect the aircraft. The bombers were painted black underneath. The USAF also began using light bombers of the B-26 Invader type, flying at low altitudes, to suppress searchlight stations. To counter MiG-15s, the Americans started using F-94B Starfire and F3D-2 Skynight night fighters.

MiG-15s had the greatest number of skirmishes with the adversary fighter-bombers. As a rule, the fighter-bombers delivered one or two massive attacks on most major targets. Two or three air groups of 150–200 aircraft flew such missions simultaneously.

Relying on the high performance of its aircraft, the USAF acted without fighter cover. At the first stage of combat actions the fighter-bombers were piston-engine F-51D Mustang and later the F-80 and F-84 jet fighters. The North Korean air force, being weak, could not meet them with a due rebuff. [Editor's note: The first American fighter-bombers in the Korean War were F-80s. Propeller-driven F-51D Mustangs came later, and only after some USAF pilots argued that jets were too fast for close air support.]

As our forces built up, the USAF fighter-bombers incurred appreciable losses. On 12 September 1951, for example, we put 80 MiG-15s into a fight, although we flew in such strength very seldom. Between Anju and Pyongyang, the MiG-15s intercepted several groups of fighter-bombers (up to 150 F-80s) that were attacking various targets while in visual contact with each other. Since the enemy had no fighter cover, the MiGs came down directly on the F-80s. The fighter-bombers ceased the strafing mission and engaged in air combat, but since they had lost 15 aircraft within a few minutes, they turned back to their bases. The MiG-15s returned to their airfields uneventfully. Only three MiG-15s sustained minor damage. The strafing operation was frustrated. [Editor's note: Records of US aircraft losses show nothing that corresponds to this claim.]

It goes without saying that not all fighter-bombers sought to evade us. Often a rendezvous with them became a short, but stubborn engagement in which we and they lost men and aircraft.

The Americans' allies in Korea did not have serious air forces. The British Royal Navy's ship-based, piston-engine Firefly and Sea Fury, operating south of Pyongyang, were used mainly as strafers and had only incidental encounters with MiG-15s—although one Sea Fury did shoot down a MiG-15.

The Australian No. 77 Squadron, flying Meteor F.8s, proved to be more martial and appeared in areas where MiGs operated.

The first engagements with the Australians showed that their aircraft were not Meteors at all. They were inferior to MiGs in all respects, and the crews' flight training level was low. Several Australian aircraft were shot down. Though the Meteors' actions were not of any military significance, in order to render justice we decided that shooting down of only Americans was not fair. For this purpose, a group of 16 MiG-15s under Lt. Col. S. Vishnyakov, the commander of this regiment, flew out and took up a holding area according to a plan initiated beforehand. When groups of fighter-bombers and F-86s appeared, 16 Meteors—practically all the surviving ones—came along behind the American pilots. Vishnyakov's group rushed forward to meet the Meters, bypassing the would-be combat area. The Australians, refusing combat, began going away one by one toward the sea and to the south but were barred by several pairs of MiG-15s. In the course of the battle, 12 Australian Meteors were brought down. The MiGs did not sustain any losses. As a result, No. 77 Squadron practically ceased to exist. [Editor's note: Records of Australian aircraft losses fail to confirm this account.]

In the second half of 1951, the Chinese and North Koreans began to be involved in combat actions. To protect strike groups, the enemy began diverting major forces against our air defences. For example, of 1,166 fighter-bombers used in six massive raids between 10 and 15 January 1953 aimed at destroying bridges at Sinuiju, 713 suppressed the air-defense system and only 453 attacked bridges. It should be added that hundreds of F-86 sorties were made to cover strike aircraft. Thus, each one strike aircraft had three or more escorting fighters.

At this time the USAF started sequential introduction of new combat aircraft in Korea. The fighter-bomber units began receiving the F-86E, the last one used in this war. [Editor's note: The F-86F (not the F-86E) was employed as a fighter-bomber and was the last Sabre version of the war.] These fighter-bombers did not give any radical advantages. MiG-15s and antiaircraft artillery went on shooting down the new aircraft equally as well as the old ones.

Following the failure of US bomber aviation, which was relegated to night operations, a perceptible defeat was also suffered by fighter-bomber aviation, mainly as a result of actions of MiG-15s flown by Soviet pilots.

American reconnaissance missions were flown by the RB-45 Tornado jet bomber and by reconnaissance versions of the B-26 and B-29 bombers. These aircraft operated over North Korean territory usually without fighter cover. When the MiG was introduced, a quiet life for reconnaissance crews ended. According to our information, all the RB-45s were shot down. MiG-15 pilots shot down RB-26s and RB-29s as well, even if they were heavily protected by fighters. [Editor's note: The RB-45 suffered problems, including lack of suitable equipment for night operation and poor prospects for crew survival in any ditching at sea. Of three deployed to Korea, one crashed en route at Midway Island, a second was shot down by MiG-15s on 4 December 1950, and the third was restricted to daylight operations near the bombline.]

The Americans soon realized that modified bombers could not be used as reconnaissance aircraft without fighter cover. Because of that, the Americans decided to fly these aircraft within groups of aircraft of similar type. This naturally decreased reconnaissance effectiveness. When the bombers shifted to night action, reconnaissance crews did the same.

All the burden associated with delivering air surveillance in the daytime in the areas that were under MiG-15 control was imposed on fighters that carried special equipment. As a rule, they flew their missions under strong F-86 protection. There were cases when a mission flown by a lone reconnaissance aircraft in MiG Alley was supported by 40 fighters.

Without any doubts the main targets for Soviet MiG-15 actions in Korea were USAF bombers and fighter-bombers. But we were simply unable to protect all of North Korea from raids by American strike aircraft. We had neither enough resources nor a free hand due to restrictions placed upon us. Nevertheless, we fought F-86 Sabres only when they prevented us from breaking through to bombers or when we encountered them by accident. I think that North Korean and Chinese pilots had a much more difficult time with Sabres.

The Americans, evaluating the tactics of the MiG-15, noted that the aircraft was rugged and had few structural limitations. The aircraft was deadly if flown by a skillful, aggressive pilot capable of using the aircraft's high performance. Our pilots shot down Col. Walker (Bud) Mahurin, a USAF group commander (imprisoned), Maj. George A. Davis, the top American ace of the war at the time (killed), and Capt. J. D. McConnell, who went on to surpass Davis as the leading American ace (after being rescued).

Our pilots N. Sutyagin and E. Pepelyaev each shot down more than 20 hostile aircraft. More than ten victories were scored by L. Schukin, D. Os'kin, G. Pulov, G. Okhay, S. Kramarenko, G. Ges', A. Smorchkov, Arkady Boytsov, D. Samoylov, S. Bakhaev, and others.

The Joint Air Army was placed in command of Chinese Gen. Lju Chjen. Our experienced Gen. D. Galunov acted as adviser. The North Korean air force was headed by Gen. Van Len. Colonel Petrachev was adviser to him.

By request of the leaders of the Joint Air Army, their formations were protected by our pilots. Soon, two divisions operating MiG-15 aircraft were brought under the command of China's Fan Tsan and Sea Byang. Conditions for training were far from the best and the linguistic barrier made coordination in fast-moving combat conditions difficult. At the same time, we all agreed on questions concerning joint operations. The Soviet pilots took in their own hands the task of parrying large forces of bombers and fighter-bombers that flew under a strong cover of the F-86s, while the pilots of the Joint Air Army were drawn in only when it was necessary.

During this war we had lost 345 MiG-15s. In most cases the pilots of these aircraft ejected safely and returned to duty. For example, the 196th FAR lost ten aircraft, but only four pilots killed.

The Americans estimated their losses in the Korean War at about 4,000 aircraft, half of these being noncombat losses. [Editor's note: American records indicate that 671 USAF aircraft were lost in the Korean war, to all causes.] We can wonder why these figures are so high. The American pilots were highly qualified and professionally trained. Their flying hours per annum were much higher than in any other air force of the world, and considerably exceeded those of Soviet pilots. US aircraft were excellent. In my time, I flew the American P-40 Kittyhawk and P-63 Kingcobra. Those were reliable aircraft, easily mastered even by pilots of average skills. The Americans operated from well-prepared concrete paved runways at airfields equipped with homing stations, radio direction finders, and complex landing systems.

I can say with certainty that Soviet noncombat losses amounted to not more than ten aircraft. If one assumes that our Chinese and North Korean allies lost twice as many aircraft, the number lost by them in noncombat conditions is not in excess of 30. This is very different from American estimates.

If one judges the American Air Rescue Service fairly, it deserves an extremely high appraisal. Pilots of the 5th AF who escaped from burning aircraft had a good chance to save themselves because the USAF rescue service was well organized and equipped. Pilots were equipped with a well-thought-out survival kit. Each pilot had a portable automatic radio beacon that served as a homing device for a rescue airplane or helicopter. The survival pack included a special mirror that was used by a pilot in distress to indicate his exact position. The pilot's seat possessed a positive buoyancy and was easily converted into a convenient raft with a sail. Besides a personal weapon, the pilots had a folding rifle, fishing tackle, a water freshener and disinfectant, dye for marking the ditching site, canned products, tobacco, and other compact objects. The crews were provided with indelible terrain maps, made on linen, and a written message for local inhabitants, containing the promise of a generous reward for rendering help.

Our air rescue service did not compare with the Americans'. We had no helicopters or light rescue aircraft. A search for pilot was made by search parties in trucks. Our pilots were not furnished with equipment to mark their locations. The survival kit of the Soviet pilot was wretched as compared with the Americans': it incorporated a pistol with two magazines, a can of condensed milk, and two or three chocolate bars. But our airmen were almost always shot down over friendly territory and help was given by local residents and soldiers of the Chinese and North Korean land forces.

But when a pilot was wounded or landed in sparsely populated mountainous terrain, his chance of survival decreased greatly. Some searches required us to organize difficult expeditions. If a pilot landed in the mountains a long distance from an airfield, it was impossible to reach him by car. We took a Yak-11 training aircraft, cut off the control stick in the second cabin, and placed a paratrooper with ampules containing blood in it. The Yak-11, covered by fighters of our regiment, arrived at the appointed place, and the paratrooper jumped out and delivered blood for the wounded pilot.

Once, rescuers found a parachute on which a pilot had landed, but he himself had vanished. In another case we failed to find either the pilot or the wreckage of his aircraft.

An American survival pack and a captured rescue helicopter were sent to the USSR for study. But no actual measures to improve our air rescue service were taken for years.

To return to the subject of figures for aerial victories, the following is an example of how thoroughly we evaluated any claim of a kill by our pilots. One of the most expert Soviet pilots, Capt. G. Ges', reported after an air battle that he had shot down an F-82 Twin Mustang fighter. According to this officer's report, he was firing at a very short distance and the hostile aircraft exploded in the air. This was confirmed by other pilots who saw the battle. However, the film of the gun camera did not confirm the outcome. The gun camera became misted in a dive. The picture got blurred. The command did not dare report this aircraft kill to higher headquarters, even though it believed Captain Ges' and his comrades. Finally, doubts were removed by a mechanic who inspected the MiG-15. Ges' had brought home a piece of a loaded magazine belt from the Twin Mustang that had become embedded in the wing of his MiG.

The Americans counted MiG kills on the basis of pilots' evidence and, as one would think, objective proof such as camera films that recorded hits on the Soviet fighters. Thus, the enemy's success was exaggerated as much as enemy air warriors' fantasy permitted. Man is vainglorious by nature, and we observed it both during the Great Patriotic War and during the Korean War. Americans were not always right when they claimed a kill based on camera film. The fact is, the MiG-15 was not vulnerable to .50cal (12.7mm) gun fire. Our pilots were protected by an armor windscreen and a 20mm armor headrest that could not be punctured by bullets. The RD-45F and VK-1 engines also had little vulnerability to American gunfire (for which, we thank the Rolls-Royce company and V. Klimov's OKB). The liners of our fuel tanks self-sealed when bullets hit them. Even in the event of multiple bullet ruptures, the MiG-15 succeeded in many cases in reaching an airfield or in continuing in combat.

Aircraft with many rupture holes were rapidly repaired by ground personnel and returned to service. In one heavy battle a MiG-15 got 120 .50cal (12.7mm) holes, but landed uneventfully, was repaired, and went into action again. The Americans' gun camera film recorded a lot of hits received on this aircraft and the Americans undoubtedly reckoned it to be a kill.

Even after an ejection, many pilots remained active. Capt. L. Schukin, one of our most valiant pilots, shot down ten hostile aircraft, was shot down, ejected and resumed flying. He shot down five more enemy aircraft, was shot down again, ejected again, and flew once more again. A similar story relates to Captain Polyansky who ejected three times but remained active.

The 64th FAC performed purely defensive tasks of protecting towns and villages, irrigation plants, roads, and the civil population, rather than military objects. You see, a peaceful population made up a considerable part of the 1.7 million Koreans killed in this war. Most of them fell victim to air strikes.

Our aviation had no offensive armament. No bombs, rockets, or napalm tanks were stored at our depots. Our complement was suitable only for defensive tasks. One can say with certainty that not a single American infantryman or seaman was killed by gunfire from Soviet MiG-15s. Simply, this was not our task. Only the 64th FAC of the VVS saw combat in Korea. A considerable number of our VVS officers were stationed in the Chinese People's Republic but were engaged in the training of Chinese pilots and never participated in combat.

I was offered a chance to return to my homeland in November 1952 after almost two years of participation in the war. Before my departure I received in Peking by Marshal Chu Te, who conveyed deep gratitude on behalf of the Chinese people to all Soviet pilots. Thus ended, for me, the third war in my lifetime.

Capt. Grigory Okhay

Grigory Okhay was born in 1917. He graduated from the Lugansk Aviation School in 1937. He saw duty in the war against Finland in 1939–1940, flying the SB bomber. During the Great Patriotic War he converted to the Yak-1 fighter. He was an instructor-pilot until 1943 when he shifted to the Soviet-German front in 1943. Okhay shot down six German aircraft. He became deputy commander of a regiment and mastered the MiG-15 during 1950. He saw service in Korea with his regiment, which was assigned to the 303rd FAD from the middle until the autumn of 1951. He flew 122 combat missions there and shot down 11 American aircraft. He was honored a Hero of the Soviet Union for victories in he skies of Korea, on 13 November 1951.

My friends and I were offered a special mission in 1950. In August, personnel of the 303rd FAD, to which my regiment was attached and which was commanded by Maj. Gen. G. Lobov, was ordered to deploy from Central Russia to the Far East to the Primorsky Territory. Just before dispatching the trains we were told at the Yaroslavl railroad station that we were being sent to China to protect North Korea. "Only volunteers are required," a senior chief said. "All who do not wish to or cannot go for some reasons should leave." Nobody left. The trains included passenger cars and flat wagons with MiG-15s, and then cars with maintenance personnel. Everything was relatively secret.

The trains crossed the border to China in March 1951. The Chinese promised to set up an air base nearer to the border and did it in an unusually short time. They chose a site in a marsh and several kilometers from the Yalu River. Ten thousand people with yokes on their shoulders and voluminous baskets attached to the yokes carried soil, sand, broken brick, cement, and other construction materials. Barefooted, in mud, sometimes in slippers and always running, they built a concrete runway about two miles, or three kilometers, long, as well as taxiways and revetments—all within one month with almost no construction equipment. Thus, Manpo airfield was ready in July 1951.

Our pilots changed to Chinese People's Volunteers uniform and, looking at one another, chuckled because really we looked very unusual in blue cotton crumple trousers, baggy field jackets, and service caps with a crumpled "pancake." All that was instead of our smart uniform and habitual top boots. There were no badges of rank. In spite of all these tricks about our secret mission in Korea, the Americans knew about our presence. Leaflets promising a guaranteed reward of $100,000 to a MiG-15 pilot-deserter to the enemy were released over Chinese airfields. [Editor's note: As indicated elsewhere, like another Russian contributor to this narrative, Okhay is confusing what he learned later with what happened at the time. The $100,000 offer was not made until 1953, long after Okhay's presence, and the leaflets were not printed in the Russian language.]

Taking off from our base, we intercepted B-29s, isolated them from escort fighters, and attacked them. At first, this was no easy task, but we became familiar with the tactics of the American aircraft and entered combat with confidence.

This was not pure self-assurance. The 303rd FAD, to which my regiment was assigned, claimed 300 enemy aircraft shot down. We did not take into account F-51 Mustangs. The worthy opponent to our MiG-15 was the F-86 Sabre. During a banked turn a Sabre could not be driven into a MiG sight; feeling danger a Sabre pilot went into a turn or banked turn that was tighter than the MiG-15 was capable of. At altitudes above 26,240ft (8,000m), the maneuvering capabilities of the aircraft were equal. The Americans preferred fighting at low altitudes where the Sabre outmaneuvered our MiG-15. Applying its efficient air brakes at altitudes up to 3,280ft (1,000m), the F-86, holding its speed down abruptly, could split-S, and its control surfaces were efficient enough to recover into level flight near the ground. If the MiG-15 had performed this maneuver, it would undoubtedly have crashed into the ground. Going down, the well-camouflaged F-86s melted into the ground clutter, while our MiG-15s were blazing in the sunshine against the ground. [Editor's note: Except for a few aircraft on an experimental basis, F-86s in Korea were not camouflaged. Rather, they were natural metal, usually with bright yellow bands on wings and fuselage.]

The MiG-15 with its higher thrust-to-weight ratio and heavy gun armament, was, beyond all question, superior to the Sabre at high altitudes in vertical-maneuver combat. On the other hand, more fuel efficient engines and a larger fuel capacity permitted the Americans to stay in the air longer.

We got our baptism of fire against the F-86s on 22 June 1951, the tenth anniversary of the beginning of the Great Patriotic War against Germany.

We were flying in a formation of eight MiG-15s from the Yalu River to the south. We were warned by GCI: four groups of Sabres were on a head-on course. The estimated location of the rendezvous was the *Sosiski* (Hot Dogs) area, a code for the Anju region. The four groups of the F-86s totaled 32 aircraft.

A command sounds: "Zamok" (Lock), meaning "tank release." The wingmen

drop fuel tanks and, just after their commander, accelerate their MiGs up to 621mph (1,000km/h) in anticipation of the battle.

We discover the Sabres just under the cloud base and nearly run into a shower of their external tanks, which they've dropped to attack us. A maneuvering battle begins. The F-86s try to articulate our formation into pairs and single aircraft persistently. And they succeed. However, they can't hit or shoot down a single aircraft. Flight commander I. Tyulyaev manages to take sight at a Sabre that has failed to release one of its external tanks and, therefore, is limited in maneuvering. Such things also happen with our MiG-15s, especially when they carry Chinese-built external fuel tanks.

Our fuel is almost exhausted. The order is heard: "Break off the battle. All return to base!" We've passed the first examination in fighting a battle. We've been driven around by the Americans, but withstood it.

One day, regiment commander Karasev fell ill. Having flown 16 combat missions, I was ordered to be a leader of a formation of 24 MiG-15s. We came to the Taysju region to intercept the enemy. We were flying along the sea coast. Exactly the same formation of American aircraft was proceeding over the sea, parallel to us. They either were showing the way to novice pilots or were waiting for something. They were "ironing" the air, the time was going by, fuel was on the wane, and we thought we would return to our base without result.

All of a sudden, six Australian Meteors appeared above the land at a low altitude. I gave a command to Masilov's two flights of eight MiGs to provide cover at 3,280ft (1,000m). The other eight led by the squadron leader stayed at 26,240ft (8,000m), and I went from 39,360ft (12,000m) down to close with the Meteors. They had been warned, and made a Lufbery circle. Each Meteor was fitted with four 20mm cannons, and while being in a circle, they protected one another well. Our first attack had failed.

We could not succeed that way, I decided, and gave the command: "Break up right, a half-roll attack!" The maneuver succeeded. Commencing fire at a distance of 1,300ft (400m), I overtook one of the Meteors with a burst from my cannons. It caught fire. Tyulyaev's, Sheverev's, and Rasorvin's pairs each shot down one aircraft. I set fire to one more aircraft. One of the six Meteors survived. Being well camouflaged, it dove to the ground, and we lost sight of it. [Editor's note: Australian records of aircraft losses do not support this account of five Meteors downed in one engagement.]

I was a formation leader in 50 combat missions and lost not a single aircraft.

The MiG-15 was an aircraft of surprising survivability. On 19 August 1951, 28 MiG-15s fought a battle with 30 F-86s, mainly in vertical maneuvers. The enemy was very skillful and dangerous. Pilots on both sides were getting the best out of their aircraft. Neither we, nor they, could shoot down a single aircraft. On completing the battle, our pilot Churkin landed at Antung with 57 rupture holes in his MiG-15.

During combat actions in Korea our regiment shot down 102 aircraft and lost 17 MiG-15 fighters and five pilots.

As for me, I flew 122 missions during which there were 86 combats resulting in 11 enemy aircraft shot down; I was never wounded, and my MiG-15 received only one bullet hole. One .50cal (12.7mm) bullet got stuck in my aileron. I am keeping this bullet still as a combat souvenir.

Col. Nikolay Zameskin

Nikolay Zameskin saw service in Korea from the second half of 1952 to the end of the war as a flight commander within the 878th FAR. In the fifteen months of his tour of duty, he made 135 combat missions during which there were 36 air combats resulting in six enemy fighters shot down and three damaged.

After the war until retiring, he served in PVOs in the north of Russia. At present, he lives in Arkhangelsk, a city in northern Russia near Arctic Circle.

Nineteen fifty-two caught me at one of the airfields of Fighter Aviation of the Baku Air Defense District.

It became known in the end of May that a unit was being formed for a special mission. Soon selection of pilots for this unit began. This was wrapped in mystery and was puzzling. Even pilots who failed to meet the requirements kept silent and said, you'll would learn what it's all about when you get called. Fourteen pilots were chosen out of several regiments of the District. This group arrived in Baku on 6 July. A representative talked to me. He said that we were going to fight, but he did not tell me where we were going to fight.

We were given the green light. We left Baku by rail on 15 July 1952. At the end of the month our train crossed the frontier. In Manchuria, we changed into Chinese People's Volunteers uniforms. Then, by Chinese Eastern Railway, we arrived at Manpo and Tapao airfields located in the area of the town of Antung.

Thus, we found ourselves in the Korean War, which has not been known to many people in the former USSR until now. We were commanded by a well-known pilot, Col. B. Yeremin, the very man to whom Saratov peasant F. Golovaty had given a fighter aircraft bought with the peasant's own cash during the Great Patriotic War.

Difficulties arose from the very beginning. Though only seven years had passed since the Great Patriotic War, many changes had taken place within that short time. We had a new generation of jet aircraft that required different tactics, but we did not know them yet. And our security restrictions, our unpublicized role in the war, meant that we were limited to flying within a restricted airspace. This did not give us a free hand in combat and limited our capabilities. All this led to early failures and losses.

By the end of 1952, the Americans began reequipping with higher-performance F-86F fighters with cannon ordnance, uprated engine, and a new wing did not readily yield to our MiG and even exceeded the latter in certain parameters. [Editor's note: Except for ten F-86F-2 aircraft armed with four 20mm cannons for prolonged combat trials in Operation Gunval, no cannon-armed Sabres served operationally in Korea.]

We opposed the F-86F with our combat formation of the *Etazherka* (Rack) type, in which squadrons (or groups) maintained vertical separation while keeping visual contact. But in the beginning we made an error: being afraid of losing one another in energetic maneuvers, pilots adhered to tight combat formations. Formations that were too close made observation of the air situation more difficult, and the Americans took advantage of it. Breaking off in small sections, they attacked suddenly and dived through our rack at maximum speed.

One incident comes to my mind. Our squadron rendezvoused with the enemy, who had established tactical superiority and who attacked us immediately. My flight was struck. The combat in-

tegrity of our formation was broken u[p], but one of my wingmen was in plac[e]. This did not help. I heard the voice of [V.] Votkin, wingmen of the second pair [of] MiGs, asking for help. After looki[ng] around, I saw at once two aircraft—ou[r] and the American. Help was rendered [in] due time: a salvo of my cannons settle[d] everything. V. brought his shot-up MiG[-] 15 to our airfield, but it was barred. M[y] wingman and I landed on an alterna[te] airfield and Votkin landed on a dirt strip.

Inspecting my aircraft, technician[s] found damage to the air intake by frag[-] ments of the exploded USAF fighte[r.] Thus, I carried the material evidence o[f] my own victory.

Very often, the enemy blocked ou[r] airfields to prevent MiG-15s from takin[g] off and, thus, to ensure safe passage fo[r] their bombers. Or the enemy laid in wa[it] for our aircraft returning after comba[t] missions and attacked them during an ap[-] proach, at a time when we were vulnera[-] ble.

One must do justice to American ac[e] pilots. They acted bravely and skillfully. [I] had a chance to watch their attack durin[g] an advanced maneuver at a diving angl[e] of 70deg.

An American ace was shot dow[n] over Tapao airfield. He had accounte[d] for 15 shot down aircraft. He came ou[t] over the airfield during takeoff of our air[-] craft, managed to shoot down one MiG[,] but he himself ran into ground fire. Th[e] American ejected and was taken pris[-] oner. [Editor's note: Possibly this is a ref[-] erence to Capt. Cecil G. Foster of the 51s[t] FIW who was credited with five kills. O[f] the three Americans who had 15 aeria[l] victories, none was taken prisoner.]

In August 1952, I managed to shoo[t] down an accomplished American pilot[.] Having detected him in a good time, [I] found myself in an advantageous posi[-] tion. The enemy used all of his skill to ge[t] out of a dangerous situation, but I stuc[k] fast to his tail following him in all hi[s] giddy maneuvers. Finally, he made an er[-] ror, and I succeeded in throwing out [a] short burst of fire. The aircraft was sho[t] down. The pilot ejected and landed i[n] mountainous terrain. He was take[n] aboard a helicopter by the American Ai[r] Rescue Service at night.

It happened that I witnessed th[e] death of my friend—air regiment deput[y] commander and Hero of the Sovie[t] Union Colonel Gorbunov—in air comba[t] above Ulumbay. The combat took place at high altitude. The aircraft were not seen from the ground. Only the drone of engines and reports of gun bursts were heard. But then, one of the aircraft started descending. It was on fire. The aircraft hit was in a turn being attacked by four fighters. As a result of this, the MiG began disintegrating in the air. All of a sudden, a white parachute canopy deployed, which meant that our pilot had been shot down. The parachute was at an altitude of not higher than 6,560ft (2,000m), and all of us who watched the pilot were glad for our friend's sake that he would be alive. The same four F-86s then began shooting at the pilot, each in turn. I always thought that if I could have helped, Colonel Gorbunov would have been alive. [Editor's note: The Soviet impression that Americans had colored parachutes is incorrect. Elsewhere in this volume is a discussion of the unwritten American rule against shooting at a man in a parachute. No treaty, law, or regulation forbids this method of attacking an enemy in wartime but American pilots claim not to have engaged in this practice.]

War is war. It cannot be fought without sacrifices. My memory is not only of the joy of successes, but also of the bitterness of defeats and the losses of my brothers, VVS officers.

The ritual of paying our last respects to killed friends was piously revered during our entire period in Korea. Often it was a purely symbolic rite of memory, but it always caused a grave and deep emotional experience.

The killed were buried in Port Arthur, near the burial ground where Russian soldiers and seamen killed during the Russo-Japanese War of 1904–1905 lie. Some time later, I went to see this graveyard and was content with the good order of this sacred place. With sadness, I read inscriptions on tombs—the names of my combat friends and fellows killed in Korea.

We learned much in the war in Korea. First, we gained experience using jet aircraft in combat missions, and though our role was not publicized, lessons reached our pilots, enriching them and contributing to their ability to master new aircraft.

After combat duty in Korea, many of my fellows in arms held prominent positions in the PVO. Among them is Lt. Gen.

D. Goryachko, an honored military pilot of the USSR.

Maj. Gen. Sergey Kramarenko

Sergey Kramarenko was born in 1923. He graduated from Borisoglebsk Military Pilots School in 1942. He flew in combat during the Great Patriotic War, during which he shot down 12 German aircraft, was wounded, and was in Germany at the end of the war. Kramarenko also flew after the war. He went on a special mission to China from April 1951 to January 1952. He saw action in Korea from December 1951. As a captain, he was commander of a squadron of the 176th FAR of the 324th FAD. He shot down 12 enemy aircraft. He was declared a Hero of the Soviet Union in 1951. After the Korean War, he graduated from the Air Force Academy, was commander of an air regiment, and then an air division deputy commander. Kramarenko retired in 1981 as deputy chief of the air staff of the Zabaikalsky Military District, with the rank of major general.

The American F-86 Sabre was the most dangerous threat to my friends and me in fights in Korean skies. Our MiG-15 and the F-86 belonged to the same aircraft class—not only similar types but similar performance. They differed only in that the MiG had a marked advantage in rate of climb at high altitude, while the Sabre was superior in level-flight maneuvering, especially at low altitudes. These advantages could not always be used. Everything depended on circumstance.

Only their armament differed, essentially. The MiG-15 was armed with three cannons, the Sabre with six machine guns. One difference was the range at which we could open fire. The MiG-15's cannons could engage targets at considerably greater distance. We could open up at a distance of about 3,280ft (1,000m).

The F-86 and MiG-15 rarely went into protracted fighting. The fight, as a rule, was decided in the first attack. It did not matter whether it was successful: after the first attack, MiG-15s reached for altitude, while Sabres rushed toward the ground. Each tried to get to the altitude where it held a distinct advantage and, thus, the air battle, having scarcely begun, faded at once.

The air battles will be described a little later. First, a word about skirmishes

with Australian Meteors. We met them somewhat earlier. The Australians used these as fighter-bombers. [Editor's note: Kramarenko refers to the Royal Australian Air Force's No. 77 Squadron, stationed at K-14 Kimpo air base, near Seoul.] They chose the railway station near the town of Ansu as a strike target. Sixteen MiG-15s of our 176th FAR took off to make the intercept. The strike group of ten aircraft was headed by regimental commander S. Vishnyakov, and the covering party was under my command. My six aircraft were above the strike group, aft and on the left.

Having the covering group in a common combat formation, we hoped to rendezvous with Sabres, and all of a sudden, we met with Meteors. This opponent, of course, was not as dangerous. There were 16 of us and 24 of them, the whole squadron. In the first attack, my pair shot down two aircraft. The other pair struck with no success. In this hit-and-run and very dynamic air battle, we shot down 16 Meteors and did not lose a single aircraft. [Editor's note: Kramarenko appears to be describing an engagement of 1 December 1951 in which 14 (not 24) Meteors fought MiGs and three Meteors (not 16) were lost, with one pilot killed and two captured. This was the costliest Australian mission of the war. While aerial victory claims on both sides were inflated, Australian records on Meteor losses are very precise.]

What was the reason for such an unprecedented success, besides the advantages of the MiG-15 over the Meteor? A surprise! What fighter pilots always try for: we found ourselves in the ideal situation. Before a strike attack during a turn on target, the enemy offered the tails of the aircraft to us without knowing it. And we took advantage.

I remember one more air battle. More than 200 aircraft were used by both sides. The enemy outnumbered us three to one. It took place on 9 April 1951. Forty-eight B-29 bombers and more than a hundred F-84s Thunderjets were rushing to the railway bridge on the Yalu River. One of the causes of our victory was their quantity.

As is usual in such a situation, the bombers were in front and the escort fighters followed them. But the latter had fallen a little behind, and our strike group with Vishnyakov at the head attacked the B-29s without hindrance, while my group, the covering party, attacked the fighters. Even though they must have seen us, our attack was a surprise. The enemy could not suppose that 20–24 MiG-15s would venture to attack such an armada. Really, the column of Thunderjets seemed to be endless. Therefore, they did not keep at required distance from each other. Being off guard, they were flying at random and spoiling fire coordination between groups.

A simultaneous and rather successful strike was made against the B-29s and F-84s. Several aircraft caught fire at once, complicating and aggravating the enemy's situation to the utmost limits. Perturbation in the formations of the Americans occurred. Bombs were falling too soon. At that moment our neighbors, the 196th FAR of our 324th FAD, commanded by Lt. Col. E. Pepelyaev, arrived unexpectedly.

The enemy had not lost his ability to resist. After my first attack, which resulted in shooting down one F-84, I attempted a corrective intended to shoot down a second F-84, but nothing of the sort happened. Making use of maneuvering advantages of the Thunderjet, the opposing pilot quickly got on my MiG-15's tail, at a distance that could be called critical, or, to be more exact, deadly.

Only a quick and very sharp maneuver could save me, and I performed it. But I pulled the control stick with such an effort and so violently that my MiG, attaining supercritical angles of attack, entered a spin. It is good that my wingman saw it. When I recovered the aircraft from a spin, the wingman joined up immediately, and we climbed upstairs, to help the group attacking the B-29s.

In that air battle we, together with the 196th FAR, shot down 12 B-29s and four F-84s. [Editor's note: A history of USAF operations in Korea indicates that only one aircraft was lost in April 1951.] We returned to our home base without suffering any losses. While attacking the B-29s, we realized that they were unable to counter MiG-15s seriously. They could deliver fire at a distance of not more than about 1,300ft (400m). Our ordnance permitted us to commence fire at a distance of 3,280ft (1,000m) and cease it at a distance of 1,640ft (500m). That means that we were able to shoot down B-29s before they could fire their .50cal (12.7mm) machine guns.

But this required skill. In order to shoot down a B-29 and not be overtaken by escort, we had to maintain a speed of 621mph (1,000km/h). At this speed, we decreased distance from 3,380ft (1,000m) to 1,640ft (500m) within 8–10sec, with the bomber's speed taken into account. These 8–10sec were all we had to take aim, depress the firing button, and shoot down our opponent. And during this time, he was maneuvering. That is why only very skillful pilots were successful in Korea.

And now, about our rendezvous with F-86s. The character of these rendezvous, I repeat, was determined by the similarity of the two aircraft types. With aircraft of similar types opposing each other, it is useless to put up a fight in any real sense, since there will be no result. That is why everything was decided in one attack.

Whether we shot anyone down or not, the opponents parted after the first attack. The Americans went toward the sea and we crossed the Yalu. Or they descended and we ascended.

But there situations in fights against Sabres, after which it was difficult to cope with oneself, difficult to believe that you were not in danger any longer.

At one time, we were taking off in flight and did not know that eight F-86s were near. They were proceeding head-on, but a little lower. Our altitude advantage favored our attack. The decision was taken to get on their tails by making a turn. But I made an error. I turned so violently that my wingmen broke from our formation and lagged behind. Worse, I did not realize it. Thinking that all of them were close by, that my wingman would protect me during the attack, I took sight of the rear Sabre.

But I suddenly had an intuition, a subconscious feeling of threat. I turned back. A Sabre was on my tail at a distance of about 328ft (100m). The American pilot did not hurry. He saw my situation. He saw that I was confident of my rear hemisphere. He intended to fire pointblank, for sure.

I made a sharp half roll. No, the word "sharp" will not do here. Actually, it was a tumbling of the MiG-15 rather than a half roll. I avoided the attack but was firmly convinced that the enemy would dog my footsteps. I threw my MiG into a dive from 26,000ft (8,000m).

There was a separate cloud hanging below. I turned back and was struck dumb. I was being followed by three F-86s. The idea flashed across my mind:

these were the very same aircraft.

It was known that an ace pilot, a colonel, a commander of an American air wing, used to fly under cover of a pair of Sabres. Operating freelance, the three would appear suddenly at places where least expected, attack at once, and go away suddenly just as they appeared. I cannot say that they kept us in fear, but they certainly made us aware of them and caused us to be on the alert. [Editor's note: Kramarenko's combat tour overlapped with the 4th FIW's Col. Harrison R. Thyng's tour and a brief overlap with the 51st FIW's Col. Francis S. Gabreski's, the only two wing commanders who were aces. Neither is well known for the tactic Kramarenko describes.]

After flying into a cloud, I started a turn immediately in order dodge any machine-gun bursts that might be sent after me. The cloud was small, and I slipped through it before I had turned 90deg. The F-86s had dropped below and ahead of me, and I attacked them at once. After they saw me, they separated: the pair went to the left while descending, and the solo ship to the right and upward. They expected me to attack those below, and in turn to be attacked by the one Sabre above me. But I upset their plan: I decided to attack the Sabre pilot who rushed upward. He had not had time yet to climb, naturally, to gain speed. Realizing my intention, the lower pair of Sabres hurried up to help. I hurriedly commenced fire at a distance of 3,280ft (1,000m). I missed my aim. I'll have time, I thought and, after closing further, opened fire again. The F-86 began smoking and started descending.

I turned back quickly. The pair were already on my MiG's tail. And they were at the point of commencing fire. I pulled the aircraft into an oblique loop. During this maneuver, it is difficult to hit the aircraft. But I made an error. I pulled it to the left instead of pulling to the right. They cut across my path, closed in, and fired.

A half roll again, a diving, a swift entrance into the single cloud, and going out. And they were already waiting for me not below, as before, but above, aft on the left and right. They were already catching up with me.

I made ten or twelve oblique loops. With ultimate G-loads. Everything went dark in my eyes. But I constantly watched the situation and terrain, gradually pulling away from the Sabres and toward the Yalu River. I could see the river at a distance of about 9mi (15km). It was time! A half roll. Diving. My direction was toward the bridge. The bridge was protected by antiaircraft gunners.

On this ill-fated 9mi (15km) leg, I understood what the MiG-15's wing heaviness meant and what an unpleasant thing it was. At a speed hardly exceeding redline, a mysterious force causes the aircraft to begin wing dropping. In order to overcome this, it is necessary to decrease speed. There seemed no way out. With each depression of my air brake button, the F-86s came nearer and nearer. One thousand meters, nine hundred, eight hundred. Suddenly ack-ack guns opened fire and cut off the Sabres.

Before landing I wanted at least to settle down a little bit. I flew three whole circles.

And what about my pilots? Well, they were unable to help me. But I did not bear a grudge. The air situation is complicated and anything can happen. In spite of anything, they are fine fellows. Having been left without a commander, they did not break off the battle; the three of them fought against eight Sabres.

Time went by, and I gained experience. I accounted for eight F-86s, two Meteors, and two F-84s. The fights were intricate and difficult, but if we set aside for a moment the way I was "squeezed" by the American ace and his team, one can say that victories became, for us, a usual thing. Unwarranted self-assurance and calm appeared, while watchfulness and a feeling of threat, though insignificant, were lost.

Again, a rendezvous with F-86s. They attacked in a pair. I attacked one aircraft and my wingman the other. It had been a custom with me to cast a glance after an attack to the rear hemisphere, from which the enemy could deliver blows. This time, I did not glance back for some reason. Having shot down one aircraft, I made a corrective turn to attack the other. At this moment, I felt my MiG-15 get hit. I am caught, I thought, but it was already late: a burst of Sabre gunfire took my controls out of action and damaged my fuel system. I had to abandon the aircraft by parachute. And though there is an international agreement banning firing at an unarmed pilot, the F-86s attacked me while I was descending by parachute. They made firing runs twice,

but did not have a chance for a third try: I had plunged into clouds. [Editor's note: No such international agreement exists. Nor did any USAF rule prohibit firing on an enemy pilot in a parachute. However, it was an American "unwritten code of ethics" not to fire upon a man in a parachute.] I landed on a volcano. Everything was all right: my head, arms, and legs were safe. I picked up my parachute and went onto a road. I was brought into a village, fed, and put into bed. The next day a car came from my unit.

Combat experience obtained by Soviet pilots in Korea may come in handy to fighter pilots nowadays. The main lesson is that one should not be off one's guard in combat, nor should one relax. One should constantly remember that there are no standard solutions for fighting in different conditions. This held true for pilots who flew MiG-15s and F-86s. It is also true for pilots who fly the MiG-29, Su-27, F-15, and F-16 fighters today.

Col. Boris Abakumov

B. Abakumov was born in 1924. He received training at the Armavir Military Pilot Training School, then graduated from the Higher Officer Instructor Pilot School. He returned to his parental Armavir School as an instructor pilot. In January 1950, he was transferred to the "Parade" Air Division at Kubinka. Abakumov flew the MiG-15 for the first time there.

He went to Korea with the 196th FAR. He flew missions as an element leader. Abakumov saw action from April 1951 until January 1952. He was shot down in January, was hospitalized, and then evacuated to the USSR. Abakumov downed five enemy aircraft in Korea (although he claims 15). He was decorated with two Orders of Red Banner for seeing duty in Korea. Abakumov was recommended for Hero of the Soviet Union. In November 1956, he was discharged from the armed forces for illness resulting from his injuries in Korea.

In the "Parade" Division, we mastered our new MiG-15s within 20 days and began flying combat missions. We young pilots were simply captivated by the charm of flying them. It was so pleasant to handle this fighter. The first MiG-15s were straightforward to fly and behaved well in the air, despite their lack of hydraulic actuators of control surfaces.

Our regiment took part in air parades

over Red Square and at Tushino, so that we were both training and accumulating flight time. By October 1950, I had already become a pilot first class.

After one of the parade air displays, selection of fighter pilots for combat in Korea began. The 324th FAD was formed by I. Kozhedub, who had been declared a Hero of the Soviet Union three times for bringing down 62 German aircraft in the Great Patriotic War. Kozhedub selected people himself. All of us realized that every pilot would play an important role in this special mission. Kozhedub understood it well too. Our team formed from different units, the average age of our pilots being 27 years.

In mid-November 1950, the first railroad train carrying maintenance personnel and combat equipment was on its way. It was followed by a "reserved" passenger train carrying flight personnel, heading for the East along the trans-Siberian line.

We were asked to be careful on all occasions, especially in the territory of Manchuria. After crossing the border with China we traveled wearing our uniform, but without badges of rank.

Our train arrived at Dunfyn. We had an airfield ready for us within two months. We began getting ready for flights, following all the rules. We started familiarizing themselves with enemy combat tactics. We studied the flight area, which was new for us, on the map and drew it from memory.

There was an impression that jet fighters were only able to mount head-on attacks. A theory that jet aircraft were never going to fight each other had taken hold among our military theoreticians and they thought they saw its confirmation at the Korean front, where the Americans did not need to put up mass air battles to gain air superiority: they had it without such fights. This theory had left its mark on our combat aircraft too. Our MiG-15s were not equipped with armored seat-backs and arm-rests that had saved many pilots during the Great Patriotic War. When battles really did become massive, we had to send for factory teams to install the armored seat-backs on the aircraft.

We pilots fighting in Korea corrected this enforced "book learning" immediately.

We used vertical maneuvers most of the time in combat, but horizontal maneuvering was not ruled out. All of the ingredients of battles fought during the Great Patriotic War were retained. It was difficult, and sometimes even impossible, to observe this combat from the ground. It spread over a huge sector of air space, both high and deep. The old factors still mattered—advantage in speed, maneuver, aimed fire, and the pilot's situational awareness and self-control. The MiG-15 had powerful armament; our smallest tactical unit, a pair of fighters, got the most out of it. But there had to be efficient coordination within the pair. A wingman could not follow his leader blindfolded, nor could he simply follow his leader in all maneuvers, the way American wingmen often did while flying in tight formation.

Only few American pairs succeeded in maneuvering. They were especially good at maneuvering while attacking a MiG-15 from astern. They used to make S-turns, gradually changing their positions relative to each other and to the target.

As a pilot who fought in the MiG-15, I assess this aircraft and the Sabre as follows.

The canopy of our cockpit did not provide as good a view as that of the F-86. The framing and double-pane windows degraded the MiG-15 pilot's visibility seriously. Moisture used to get frozen between double panes, which led to zero sideways view above 23,000ft (7,000m). Frost became the enemy's ally. Fortunately, our technicians overhauled our canopies to make them more airtight, and every day they blew out the space between glass plates with compressed air. Sometimes, this was done after every sortie.

A Sabre pilot sat high in his cockpit. We saw their shoulders up to the chest. Their canopy was of single-glass frameless construction, much larger in size than that of our MiG-15. There was glare on our double-pane canopy transparencies, even from a flight jacket to say nothing of strong reflections from chrome-plated handles and even from painted instrument panels, so that the eyes got very tired.

The F-86 cockpit interior was frosted grey and green and did not cause specks of light on the canopy. The canopy itself was shaped not to provoke glare visible to the pilot.

Ejection could be effected from the Sabre by both seat handles and not by only a right-hand handle, as on our aircraft. If a bullet had been put into my right hand, I would have reached across with my left hand and would have broken my back during ejection. We had no anti-G suits, while the Sabre pilots wore them all the time.

The air brakes on our aircraft were too small to be effectively applied for deceleration when fighting. The air brakes on the Sabre had a large area, and the American pilots used them often, even when diving. The F-86 wing was provided with leading-edge slats that helped it to maneuver at high angles of attack. We had no such capability and so the MiG-15 yielded to the Sabre in the horizontal plain.

The F-86 engine casing was made of an easily cracked material. MiG-15 engines were extremely survivable, as was the entire aircraft. Besides, the MiG-15bis engine had a high thrust and, as a result, a high thrust-to-weight ratio.

The F-86 radio used 12 channels and was more advanced than that installed on MiGs.

Enemy pilots wore crash helmets protecting the head from fragments. We flew wearing leather headsets.

In combat at high altitude we had to breathe cold 100-percent oxygen. It makes the throat dry and its low temperature affects the respiratory tract.

And now let us revert to the events of 1951. Two days after we came to Dunfyn, MiG-15s were delivered. The aircraft came later than we did, although they had left Kubinka earlier. We assembled the aircraft quickly, removed our Soviet markings, and put on the North Korean ones and then we proceeded to training flights. It was winter. It was very cold in fighter cockpits. The ground got cracked by frost. That is why we were relieved after standing alert for half an hour. The MiG cockpit was small, and to sit there in fur clothes, especially when awaiting a battle, was uncomfortable. So we sat in our cockpits in light, leather jackets in freezing weather.

North Korean pilots converted to MiG-15s at this airfield. Not all the Koreans strained to be in action. Some made gross blunders intentionally or tried to drag out training and thus to delay a rendezvous, fatal to them, with American aircraft.

On 12 February we took into the air and headed for Mukden, where we refueled the aircraft and then made for Anshan. The airfield had been built there long ago, by Japanese. The taxiways were covered with asphalt. There were reinforced concrete shelters for several fighters. The airfield was equipped with a night flight system which we used actively. In this new place we stayed on alert.

On our first day at Anshan airfield we met pilots who were returning home. This was the regiment that had been sent to China from Kubinka a year ago. They had fought dozens of battles with the Americans in Korean skies and told us what we were to expect.

In order to assess the situation of the first group of Soviet pilots, I should say that they were declared a Hero of the Soviet Union for shooting down three or four aircraft, were decorated with the Order of Lenin for 30 combat sorties, and were given the Order of Lenin for 120 combat sorties. That is a sign of the difficulty of those first fights with the Americans.

We did not stay in Anshan long. Combat became more intense. New groups of F-86s appeared. The 64th FAC decided to commit our division to battle. Early in April we flew to the Korean border and engaged in combat at once. Some of our groups met enemy aircraft even before landing at our home field, Antung. One of our pilots even attacked an RB-45 American reconnaissance aircraft, but he had forgotten to charge his cannons and "fired" on it with his gun camera. The target did not wait for the MiG's cannons to place fire on it but headed south quietly.

Landing on the airfield at night we were asked to analyze the flying day together with the pilots of the regiment that was based there for its final day and the next day was to take our place at Anshan. On that day, the Americans damaged the truss of the only railway bridge over the Yalu River, through which Chinese and North Korean troops were supplied. The bridge was repaired with materials at hand within 24hr. This experience pointed to the tasks assigned to us—to gain air superiority in the region, to provide air cover of strategic objectives, and to protect Chinese regions adjacent to North Korea.

At that moment, we had the two-regiment 324th FAD. Each squadron had only eight aircraft.

Division airfields were located on the Liaodong Peninsula where the air divisions that protected Port Arthur were based. Airfields were being built on Korean territory, but neither we, nor the Chinese, nor the North Koreans could take advantage of them because the enemy destroyed them rather quickly.

During the first two months we flew combat missions in squadrons (in eights) and, frequently, in an incomplete force (in sixes) to fight against any force of enemy aircraft. Sometimes we made sorties in regiments, but each squadron initiated its own combat and broke into pairs as the American side outnumbered us at least three to one. The American pilots could freely withdraw from action to their safe area over the sea where we were strictly prohibited from going. We were also forbidden to fly beyond Pyongyang, but in the heat of battle it sometimes happened.

Of no small importance was the position of the sun, a camouflage factor. It was always on the sea side where the enemy grouped. In addition to this, the American aircraft had the appropriate camouflage color. As for our aircraft, they glittered in the sun and reflected sunbeams to a great distance. [Editor's note: Two Russian pilots tell us in this volume that American fighters were camouflaged. They were not.]

The day after our relocation, we had to meet Sabres above the bridge. When in the air, we saw that a narrow bridge to pass motor transport in one direction had been attached to the railway bridge. That day, there were multiple cloud layers with low-level clouds at about 6,560ft (2,000m). Enemy aircraft broke out of the clouds and, flying beneath them, combed the battle area at high speed. Then they plunged into the clouds again. Our group was ordered to protect the bridges. We were also commanded neither to enter the clouds nor to engage in combat with the fighters. The Americans knowing the capabilities of our P-3 radars came in close, four-aircraft formations to the bridge, simulating bombers in speed and formation. And our ground radars actually took them for bombers. Hence, I. Kozhedub ordered us not to get into action against the fighters but to wait for a bomber raid. But there were no bombers.

In this first fight, I saw a pair of Sabres in the clear. I directed my fighter

to them, but they rushed into the clouds again and I saw them no more. This time the enemy did not meet my eye again, but from intense communication I understood that somebody was shooting. Litvinyuk even made out their color well: they were of dirty-green color with white stripes on the wing surfaces near the fuselage. Our first meeting with the enemy had taken place.

After this first combat sortie, Kozhedub drew our attention to the fact that a pair should be indivisible, and if one happened to lose a leader or wingman, one should make a new pair.

On 6 April in the afternoon, the second squadron of eight aircraft, under B. Bokach, took to the air. I was a member. When aloft, we were tasked to meet a force of enemy fighters coming from the sea side. We met them on a head-on course over the coast. The first eight F-86s flew by without changing their course. Two four-aircraft formations above us attempted to box us in, using a half-roll to get on our tail. We zoomed immediately and formed a sheaf of pairs flying to different sides. Vertical air fighting began. At that moment one more group of enemy aircraft was noticed approaching. We were informed of it by GCI.

Shelomonov's squadron took off to help us. It chased the enemy all the way to Pyongyang. My wingman G. Loktev and I fought four Sabres. I sat on one pair's tail and raced after them trying to hit the wingman when he bottomed out in recovery from a dive. Our automatic sight did not operate at such G-loads. I had to sight the target and correct aiming via a tracer streak so that the nose of my MiG-15 covered the target. All the time, the shells were passing between the enemy airplane's nose and its left wing. I was firing the 23mm cannons. To provide a better scattering and more complete coverage of the target, I had to swing my aircraft nose a little using my pedals. The enemy aircraft rocked due to bursts of my shells, but continued flying. Later, American pilots who were taken prisoner said that some Sabres used to come home with up to nine holes made by 23mm shells.

The other pair of the four-aircraft formation was firing at me on a crossing course. Small, dove-colored tracers passed by. I was not hit, but my wingman received a wing hole. Being unable to

stand this whirligig, the enemy made a violent maneuver almost on top of a left, oblique half loop and evaded my fire at low speed.

My throat was dry. My face was flaming. My left hand was depressing the transmitter button for some reason and I was feverish. I calmed after the skirmish and saw eight Sabres in front of me. They were flying toward our airfield. I looked around. There was no my wingman near, and I did not know why. Then I realized that he had fallen behind during one of the oblique loops. I rushed after the eight aircraft ahead of me. On my right, A. Litvinyuk's pair was fighting, and to my left there was also a roundabout, with B. Bokach's pair in combat.

I was closing with the eight aircraft slowly. Within the effective distance of fire, I switched off the automatic-sight system and offset the aiming point above the target by the length of the enemy aircraft fuselage since the target was moving away and the MiG was losing its speed due to recoil of the cannons. I threw a long burst of fire from the 23mm cannons into the leader. The tracer streak directed toward the target and locked on it. The F-86 made a rocking motion, and there seemed to be a white explosion on its left wing. Foggy vapor trailed after the aircraft. Rolling to the left, the enemy broke through its formation down and went toward the sea while descending quickly. The other Sabres followed it. *Well, I think, I have hit the commander,* I thought. Later, we were told that the Sabre, piloted by USAF Major Crown, had bellied in near Pyongyang. He did not have enough fuel to reach his base; I had hit his aircraft fuel tanks. He was taken prisoner. The F-86 was disassembled for carriage in two trucks, but American attack aircraft smashed them on their way to our airfield.

On 12 April 1951, I was involved in breaking up a raid mounted by 150 fighters and 48 B-29 bombers.

My four aircraft came up above the bomber formation and rushed into an overhead attack at once. I took sight of two B-29s at a time. My distance for opening fire was 3,600ft (1,100m), and for breaking off the attack 1,300ft (400m). Distances for opening fire in subsequent attacks were half of this.

I saw my shells ripping up the surfaces of both aircraft. The B-29s jettisoned their bombs before reaching their target. One of the bombers turned away from its bomb run sharply and made for our airfield while firing from all turrets. There was nobody to protect the airfield. I pointed my aircraft at the enemy immediately. I closed on the B-29, offset the aiming point ahead, covering the target with the nose of my aircraft completely. I threw a burst of fire from all the cannons and lowered the aircraft nose so that I could see the target and my tracer streak. An undershoot: the tracer streak was 10ft (3m) behind the B-29's tail, and I saw my shells flying to the concrete runway of my home airfield.

During my attack, I passed the bomber's tail. My aircraft was turned over by the propeller slipstream. I made a corrective inside turn and re-attacked. I did not see my wingman. I made an aiming correction and shot away all remaining ammunition into the B-29's tail. This went to pieces before my eyes. The crew abandoned the aircraft and descended by parachutes.

The battle continued, but I had no ammunition. I. Kozhedub ordered from the ground, "Don't break off combat!" I made false attacks on enemy fighters. While I was rushing in vain after F-84 Thunderjets, a pair of Sabres got on my tail. They poured fire on me from their machine guns. I made a violent half roll to pull out of the dive. The F-86s dived and pursued me, dropped down when recovering from the dive, and lagged behind a little. I rushed into the antiaircraft-fire area. Ack-ack guns cut off the Sabres, and I landed on our airfield. After the landing my technician found eight holes in my MiG-15. I was given Kozhedub's MiG for the next sortie. His aircraft was of smoke color, and during the second battle on that mad day the Sabre pilots looked at it cautiously.

In May I was awarded the Order of Lenin. In the same month we started receiving the more advanced MiG-15bis with power-assisted controls to which one had to get accustomed. We were more self-reliant in our old fighters because a loss in speed in air combat could be determined by the feel of the control stick rather than by looking at the instruments, as one had to do now.

Just in the first fight several pilots had fallen into a spin on the new MiGs. I went into a flat spin. All this happened in a battle, with Sabres actively fighting us. I managed to recover from the spin only near the ground. The aircraft had been deformed by G-force during the spin recovery and became difficult to handle. But still I got to the airfield and made a safe landing.

In July the USAF began to operate the latest all-weather two-seat F-94B fighter for reconnaissance flights in continuous cloud. They penetrated deep into Chinese territory and reached Mukden. Eight F-94Bs went to Mukden, made their reconnaissance mission, and then were returning. To intercept them, ten MiG-15s took off under E. Pepelyaev's command. I was in the closing pair. We broke through the clouds together, in tight formation. We proceeded at maximum speed and met the F-94s. We maneuvered to attack them, broke into pairs, and attacked the enemy from different sides. It was Pepelyaev who shot down the first aircraft. He sawed off the F-94's fin with a burst of fire. I sighted the leader and shot at him. My shells had their effect. The F-94 gradually tilted to the left and went toward the ground with its nose down. Only one of the eight F-94Bs managed to survive in this battle.

On this occasion the Soviet newspapers reported that Chinese pilots had fought a battle and shot down seven out of eight aircraft of the aggressor. We smiled, as we knew the combat capabilities of Chinese pilots very well. [Editor's note: American records do not confirm anything resembling the F-94B mission to Mukden described here, the use of the F-94B for reconnaissance, or the loss of seven aircraft in one engagement. No more than one F-94B was reported as lost during any engagement during the Korean War.]

Often the Chinese pilots were self-confident and flew off without our protection. Frequently, it ended in tragedy for them. One day they flew off independently without giving notice. As a result, they lost their regimental commander, a good pilot, one of the few they had. This regiment came across a force of B-29s over the sea. The commander of the regiment cut speed rapidly, almost to that of the bombers, to attack them. The other Chinese MiG-15s rushed by at a high speed, forsaking him. Sabres were running after him. The regimental commander attacked three B-29s in turn, and according to the Chinese, downed them, but he himself was also attacked and shot down by an F-86.

It occurred over the sea. His MiG-15 ran into the bottom. When the tide ebbed, its tail was seen projecting over the water surface. This was the very MiG-15 that was taken out by the English ship.

One day when returning to base after a mission, we saw nine Chinese Tu-2s below. We landed on the airfield, and some time later three riddled Tu-2s landed. Six of them had been shot down by Sabres that attacked them over the sea when the Chinese made an attempt to bomb islands occupied by the Americans. Well, the Chinese command should have contacted our control tower and asked us to cover the area where the Tu-2s were to operate.

In September 1951, I was given my second Order of Lenin. In the autumn of 1951 we operated against F-80s. We found them in the area of Nampo and rushed into combat. I got on a pair's tail and took aim on number one. His wingman was flying in tight, left-echelon formation. My wingman, N. Vermin, was following me. He even sustained a hole drilled in his fin by my ejected cartridge cases. Half of the left portion of his aircraft fin was cut, but it did not fall off.

My sight was set to automatic mode, but the shells went to the forward corner of the left wing-to-fuselage joint, rather than along the cockpit center where I was aiming. Evidently, the enemy was slightly slipping to the right. The enemy wingman did not make any maneuvers and simply copied all the actions made by the leader. After my second burst of fire, he just remained rolling into a left turn but, instead of climbing, began to fall. His wingman was going after him as though attached to him. *What is this radio-controlled aircraft*, I wondered. A pair of MiGs behind and below my aircraft started shooting at the wingman from a short distance. Both F-80s were destroyed.

Such a picture of doom had a bad effect on me. What had happened to the American pilots? Why had they not tried to evade our attack? I decided that they had simply not seen us. Having driven the F-80s away and having downed five aircraft, we came back to our base without any losses.

Early in November 1951 we flew an independent mission with four fighters, led by Pepelyaev. I was going in a pair with A. Ovchinnikov. We came to the Anju region and did not encounter F-86s there. Then we saw Thunderjets toiling with might and main below us: napalm was burning on the ground, ground targets being attacked. Pepelyaev put his MiG-15 into a dive, and we followed him without breaking up the combat formation.

My wingman and I reached the altitude where the F-84s were operating in a close formation. When the Thunderjets saw us, they began breaking off to head toward the sea. Pepelyaev began to fire at one of them. I got into my sight another one that was descending and fleeing at full speed. I opened fire at a distance of 2,600ft (800m). My tracers hit the F-84 at the cockpit. The enemy aircraft rolled left, dropped its nose, and crashed into the sea. The sea was not deep at this location, and the aircraft tail projected up through the water. Our group broke off, took up formation, and went home. Little fuel was left. We had ignored the ban on flying over the sea.

Air battles near the stratosphere were to our advantage. A. Mitusov told me that half of his kills were achieved at high altitudes. This was because he mostly flew cover. Actions performed by a covering group are specific: one should fly above the enemy during any combat. The cover group was responsible for fighting enemy "hunters" who stayed high during combat.

In October 1951, our medical board offered many pilots of our division the chance to return to the USSR. Because of permanent strain on the nerves and physical strain from combat actions, many of our pilots felt a heartache that did not cease even after quite some time. Some pilots accepted the offer. Some remained, on I. Kozhedub's request. Many pilots who left had to be given medical aid. We were exhausted from constant combat.

In January 1952, pilots of the 97th FAD (PVO) came as replacements. They arrived without maintenance personnel. We were ordered to give our technicians to the newcomers, and this cut to the quick. Kozhedub expressed his dissatisfaction. For this, he fell into disgrace. Still, we did our best to train our replacement pilots as efficiently as possible. We lectured them on combat use of the MiG-15 in this theater, on enemy tactics, and on details of action against different types of enemy aircraft.

Air fighting continued. On 7 January, I flew out with the last pair to provide cover for the leading pair of regimental deputy commander A. Mitusov. Our group was to climb to high altitude and hit the Sabres. The Sabres were in force. They entered a radar dead area, let six aircraft go into an inversion zone as a decoy, and the others assumed position under and above them.

We ran this mission in eight pairs. My wingman, one of the newcomers, dropped behind me in flight. I continued to protect Mitusov's pair alone. Our three pairs were going deep into Korean territory at 39,360ft (12,000m). We saw 12 F-86s proceeding slightly higher. As soon as we met them, they made a half roll and tried to attack us from astern. We entered a climb gradually and left the enemy below. Eight more Sabres came up on a head-on course above. We had not regained the speed we had lost during the climb. Immediately these F-86s, making a half roll, got on our tail. All eight aircraft rushed toward me. Assuming responsibility for these aircraft, I distracted their attention from Mitusov's pair. Now, his pair could climb and attack and thus help me. But as it turned out, the third enemy echelon was flying at a higher altitude. Four aircraft were there, and Mitusov and his wingman engaged them. They shot down one Sabre and the others were forced to descend. Now they were able to help me. All this time, I had been fighting eight aircraft alone.

I managed to get rid of an enemy pair that had been sitting on my tail, proceed to an attack, and commence precision fire at the leader. Breaking off the attack, I momentarily lost consciousness due to high G-loads, and when my sight was restored I could not see the results of my attack.

Before I had time to turn back to look about, bullets began pattering on my left wing. My left hand that was resting on the throttle control lever was struck and for some reason became very heavy. A grey shroud appeared before my eyes. I moved my controls to the right abruptly in order to escape the fire. The cockpit decompressed, I felt it in my ears. I looked back, and the pair whose fire I had just escaped was following me. I performed a maneuver and attacked, but was hit by .50cal (12.7mm) bullets fired by another pair that I had not seen. The enemy aircraft broke down into pairs and waited where I would break off the attack, to kill me finally.

The instrument panel in my cockpit was burning. It had sustained a hit by an armor-piercing, incendiary bullet. I pulled the control stick, but the aircraft did not obey. The controls had failed. My aircraft was climbing with a left roll. The next burst broke my left arm humerus. I got a blunt blow on my shoulder and saw white bone fragments flashing from the wound, and I decided to eject. I took my immobile left hand into the right one, removed it from the throttle control lever, and put it on my knees. I was unable to place my legs on the ejection seat pedals; I made use of my strong right hand to do this. I swung the ejection seat guard from the right side and jettisoned the canopy. I rolled up as much as possible and depressed the seat ejection firing lever.

I was pressed into the seat sharply. A clang was heard on the left seat rail guide: the Sabre's bullets seemed to have damaged it. I ejected out of the cockpit and began falling.

My strong right hand groped for the seat harness safety pin and unlocked it. My legs hung down at once and separated from the footrests. The seat came off. Now, I could deploy the parachute. (At that time our parachutes were not equipped with automatic devices.) I pulled the parachute ripcord handle, but only managed to take it out of its pocket when everything went dark before my eyes.

I released the ripcord handle and, groping for the ripcord, began pulling it out by displacing my fingers and pressing the ripcord with my thumb from above. Some time later I felt a jerk, and the parachute opened. During all this time I had lost altitude which made my position easier as I had ejected at some 39,3600–45,900ft (12,000–14,000m), and the oxygen mask had been torn from my face. It was dangling on my breast but, nevertheless, some oxygen seemed to get into my lungs. Everything taken together saved me. I was lucky.

After the parachute opened, I saw a pair of Sabres running in at a 90-degree banked turn. They had not turned enough, and seemed to have overrated their maneuverability. My parachute canopy remained inside their turn radius. The Sabres rushed by and went away. My further descent was quiet.

I landed (if it may be called a landing) on a steep volcano slope. During landing, I struck my head against stones.

Evgeny Pepelyaev was honored with the title of Hero of the Soviet Union and with combat awards for his service in Korea.

I was picked up by a Korean; I stayed with them two days. They did what they could to help me. On the third day, a car came to take me to a hospital. My left arm was to be amputated, but this turned out to be unnecessary.

In February 1952 when our unit left for the USSR, I was still not movable.

Combat continued. Our replacement pilots were already fighting. Success did not attend them, though. Two months later they were withdrawn to the second line.

PVO Commander P. Zhigarev asked Kozhedub three times why things were in a bad way with the 97th FAD. The latter answered that we did all that we could. We had left the maintenance personnel and did our utmost to prepare the pilots.

To study the situation, Marshal E. Savitski and F. Agaltsov were sent over there with an inspection team.

All were at a loss. Hospital chief A. Gorelik asked me: "What's the matter? The Sabre pilots were afraid of you. Now

they are just walking over our heads." I had to parry the question. He himself understood the situation. His hospital was full of pilots from the 97th with their old diseases rather than with battle injuries.

The pilots that had come as our replacements were from the 97th FAD, which was inspected by Savitski and Agaltsov. The marks they gave to the pilots in combat training had been the best. And now it was really very awkward, with both of them sent to Korea to make an inspection.

"Regimental honor" made them find a way out of this ticklish situation. They decided to do the following: delay conferring decorations upon pilots of Kozhedub's 324th FAD, which would result in decreasing the contrast when comparing combat operations; inspect the work of the 324th's predecessors, though the latter had left the battle area long ago; find fault with the work of the 324th so that the relative performance of the 324th and the 97th was not so strikingly in contrast.

This energy and quick wits should have been used for training of the relieving pilots.

All this proved to have been programmed, which caused a derisive and mistrustful attitude toward our activities, which fed unfavorable talks and gossip concerning us. Up to the present moment things like this are sometimes heard: "Well, tell me how you got out of there."

All these years after my battle injury, I have had to look after my health. I have not given up the belief that after all, justice will triumph and the good name of the 324th FAD will be restored. The guarantee for that is the combat activity of our pilots, the living and the dead. Glory to the living and everlasting memory to the dead.

Col. Evgeny Pepelyaev

E. Pepelaev, a retired colonel, was born in 1918. He graduated from Odessa Military Pilot School in 1938. E. saw service in the 29th Red Banner Fighter Regiment stationed in the Far East, and flew I-16 fighters. He became deputy commander of a squadron of the 300th FAR in 1940.

For the entire war, he was in the Far East where he bombarded the leadership with requests to shift him to the Western front, but there was the million-strong Japanese Army on our border and good fighter pilots were needed there, too. He saw action against Japan in August 1945.

[Editor's note: American readers will remember that the USSR entered the war against Japan only in its final month.] After graduating from Command Personnel Training courses at Lipetsk VVS Training Center in 1946, he was sent to serve in the "Parade" Division based then at Kubinka, where he was assigned as deputy commander of the 196th FAR. There, Pepelyaev became engaged in operational evaluation and field tests and became familiar with new aircraft. The Yak-9 with reversible propellers as well as Yak-17 and La-15 jets passed through his hands. The regiment received its first MiG-15s at the end of 1949. Pepelyaev got familiar with this aircraft very quickly. From April 1951 to January 1952, he fought in Korea as commander of the 196th FAR with the rank of colonel. He was the top-scoring Soviet ace in Korea and shot down 23 American aircraft.

Pepelyaev was declared a Hero of the Soviet Union in April 1952. On returning to his homeland, he saw service in an air defense division as its deputy commander. He graduated from the General Staff Academy in 1956. He was commander of the 133rd FAD. After deactivation of the division, in the early 1960s he was chief of aviation of the Air Defence Corps, then served in the command center of the PVOs. After service in Korea, he mastered the MiG-19 and Yak-25. At present he is on the retired list and lives in Moscow.

The first pilots of the 29th FAR based in Kubinka who were sent to Korea in August and September 1950 did not know that they were going to take part in real fighting until reaching the very border of the USSR with China. This regiment and one more, deployed from Kubinka to China in February and March 1950, saw the first fights against American aircraft. Some time later, the 151st FAD under Sapozhnikov was transferred there. This group fought rather successful battles with the USAF F-80s, F-84s, and F-51s. Then Sabres appeared and the Soviets began to suffer losses because American pilots did not yield to ours and sometimes exceeded us in performance. The Soviets began evading and breaking off combat.

When we arrived to replace our predecessors in March and April 1951, our situation was to some extent one of flight and panic.

The commander of the VVS of the

Moscow Military District, V. Stalin, came to Kubinka in November 1950, gathered officers around him, and told it straight: "Whoever is not a coward will go to China," he said. "Volunteers are wanted."

A two-regiment division with fewer pilots and aircraft began to be formed out of the three-regiment division at Kubinka. I. Kozhedub became commander of the 324th FAD. I was offered a chance to command the 196th FAR. At that time, I had 2,000 flying hours and had flown the MiG-15 for about a year.

Before being dispatched to China, MiG-15s were disassembled, packed in containers, and loaded on railway flat cars. Trains were brought directly to Kubinka. Our departure was not a parade, but it was not concealed from wives and colleagues. It was known in the garrison that we were going to Korea. The only subterfuge was that shoulder stripes were removed from our uniform. Freight trains with equipment arrived first in China, followed by passenger trains with pilots.

We arrived at a rear airfield of Dunfyn, located about 186mi (300km) from the Korean border There, we assembled and flew out our MiG-15s, painted with markings of the North Korean air force. My aircraft operated in Korea as No. 778 or 767, I do not remember exactly, and the nose of my MiG was red and the aircraft had no camouflage whatsoever.

At the beginning of the war we operated MiG-15s with the RD-45F engine and OSP-48 (SV) sight, but from the summer of 1951 deliveries of MiG-15bis aircraft began.

Pilots who had already encountered F-86s reported that the American fighters were up to the mark and that the American pilots' proficiency was of high standard.

Here, I understood that my air regiment was not ready for the coming fight. Ninety percent of my pilots had fought in the Great Patriotic War toward its end, and each had scored one or more kills. But now the enemy was different. And my pilots had lost their combat awareness. When a man loses touch with war for several years, marries, has children, and a permanent dwelling, he is no longer a warrior. One loses combat skill and savage instincts, both necessary in combat. In my group, 10 percent were young men who yielded nothing to the veterans and even exceeded them in some ways.

I drew up a program to train my pilots. Not everybody in the 64th FAC (under Maj. Gen. I. Belov) supported it, but I was given a go-ahead and began preparing for future actions.

In just days, pilots began growing roots in the MiG-15. When MiGs rushed over Dunfyn at maximum speed at 328ft (100m), the commandment asked: "Who authorized this?" I answered, "War."

Training was carried out often, and all kinds of combat formations were practiced. A pair fought against a pair, and a flight against a flight. December through March passed with this strain. We were striving for the American standard.

In mid-March, I challenged I. Kozhedub to simulated combat with his 176th FAR. My pilots won the battle over their brother regiment completely. To my mind, no other Soviet unit underwent so much combat training in MiG-15s.

In the early 1950s, the VVS stressed training under bad weather conditions. Flights were often made at night in bad weather, landing with radar aids. The instrument landing system was being mastered. But, besides all these useful things, a combat pilot, especially a fighter pilot, must be able to fire and turn in the air in order to shoot down the enemy and not be shot down.

Our high-ranking military authorities did not care much. It was thought that the real war had passed, nothing serious was in prospect, and flight safety came first. One could lose not only rank but one's life if an aircraft went down

I believe that Soviet pilots in Korea before and after us were insufficiently prepared for combat. Pilots of our 324th FAD were adequately trained, and the pilots of my 196th FAR had the best training of all of them. I am not boasting. Very simply, we prepared to fight. Compared with us, the 176th FAR had poor combat instruction, though they trained for three or four months, first in Dunfyn and then at Ang-shan like us.

I said it openly both during and after the Korean war. This caused open hostility toward me by Marshal E. Savitski, the PVO commander who disapproved my second gold star. He and his deputies sent to Korea pilots of PVO regiments who were not ready. These pilots were drilled in flying cross-country, in clouds, at night, but not in aircraft interception.

Early in 1952, we were replaced by the 97th Air Defense Division deployed

from the environs of Moscow. Most pilots of this division were first-class pilots, but they had no idea how to fight.

At the end of March 1952, the situation became more complicated. The 196th FAR was deployed to Antung where we engaged in our first combat with the Americans. By that time we had accumulated considerable flight time. The first April skirmish proved our methods of battle training. Our pilots returned to base after the first battle with no losses, though without a single victory. The 176th FAR lost three aircraft, one of which, after being hit, exploded at the airfield. I gathered my squadron commanders after the first action and instructed them as follows: if it is not urgently required, attacks must not be staged in unfavorable situations. The main thing now is to study American tactics and search for their weak point. As for our MiG-15, it possessed advantages; why not take advantage of them?

And now, some words about the aircraft. The first MiG-15s we brought to Korea were worse than both F-86s and MiG-15bis. The latter was superior to the F-86 in vertical maneuverability at high altitude. It behaved well at altitudes from 19,680 to 32,800ft (6,000–10,000m) where most fighting occurred. The Sabre could break off combat by diving easily, and it turned better. Because of this, I had lost my wingman, Z. Larionov.

I shot down an American Sabre pilot. He ejected, but broke his leg on landing and was taken prisoner. I asked the reconnaissance department to ask him how much time it took the F-86 to bank at different altitudes. He gave some information but later we found from combat experience that he had lied.

In July 1951, we flew a six-plane combat mission. Six F-86s were ahead of us. Our position was favorable. Knowing that I was protected by my wingman, and that Captain Nazarkin's flight was high astern, I attacked. I got involved in a turn with a Sabre. But Nazarkin's flight could not provide cover for us. Later he explained that he had lost sight of us because of the sun. Maybe it is so. I do not know. The Americans, having better turning characteristics and knowing that we had no protection, got at my wingman at once. We could not even bury Larionov. His aircraft fell into the Yellow Sea.

And immediately, a burst of fire hit my MiG-15. The second pair ran in from

Evgeny Pepelyaev with his wingman after the Korean war. A MiG-15 is in the background.

the right. Nazarkin kept silent. I realized that help would not be rendered. Well, what was the use of an air victory then? I threw my aircraft into a spin and went down. An F-86 above me spiraled down, but the pilot had not enough skill to reach me. I rushed into the cloud, turned my aircraft near the water, and proceeded to our airfield. And Nazarkin did not fly any longer; he was sent back to the USSR. So we knew now, the hard way, that the Sabre made banked turns better than the MiG-15.

We had more powerful armament, and they possessed a better sight—a radar rangefinder coupled to an optical sight. A pilot in our aircraft introduced correction into his gun sight manually, by eye. During abrupt maneuvers, the sight became unstable. Actually, all the fights by our MiG-15s were with the gun sight operating in the conventional collimating mode.

I liked the MiG-15's 37mm cannon, despite its low rate of fire. In the hands of a skilled pilot firing at short distance, the cannon was good against both fighters and bombers. It was bad when it jammed, leaving only the NS-23 or NR-23.

The American .50cal (12.7mm) guns acted on our MIG-15s like peas. Our aircraft would return to airfields with 40–50

bullet holes. The Americans claimed them as shot down, while our pilots were safe and sound. The MiG-15 was more survivable than the Sabre: our pilot was protected by the engine from astern, and the VK-1 or RD-45F engine itself was more survivable than the J47 on the Sabre.

A former pilot of mine, Lieutenant Pavlovski, came to see me in Antung. He told me how Sabres had shot him down. They swarmed around him. He turned to the right. They fired tracers. He turned to the left. They shot tracers. Thus, they were holding him and wanted to lead him to their airfield. Then they started practicing in firing at him. His VK-1 malfunctioned. The pilot made up his mind to descend and then they were really shooting at him. He ejected. The MiG's survivability was fantastic. We must thank Mikoyan designers for that.

But let's return to everyday combat life. The Americans were forbidden to fly across the Yalu River, and we to go south of the Pyongyang–Wonsan line or out to sea. But both we and they ignored these bans. The Americans came over the airfield on the day of our arrival at Antung. It was as though they challenged us to action and examined what sort of lads had appeared and what we were worth. By June when we were accustomed to the situation, we too began neglecting these bans. We flew both above the sea and even across the Pyongyang–Wonsan line. As for me, I got in trouble since, unfortunately, I lost a pilot over the line. War is a more intricate thing than all bans, and often one must assume responsibility. War is war.

The first victory over F-86s was natural. We had not been hasty and had gained experience. I had been learning myself and teaching my subordinates.

In one of these fights a Sabre pilot was breaking off a regular attack with daredevil stuff. He made a banked turn just under my MiG-15's nose. The result was not long in coming: My MiG-15's cannons riddled my first Sabre.

And now about a notable fight in the autumn of 1951, as a result of which we captured an intact F-86.

The battle was violent. I put into the fight the entire 196th, meaning 24–26 aircraft, against the F-86s. Our fraternal 176th was flying below. I called them: "You see the battle. Come and help us!" They kept silent and slipped toward the

sea. At that moment, I hit one Sabre. As a result of a forward-cone attack, I too was hit, but sustained only one rupture hole. Then we began to use our combat training. I had a concept for attack that I had developed before the war, and I used it.

I made as if to get into a combat left turn, but during an oblique loop maneuver I turned my MiG to the opposite side. The F-86 pilot had fallen for the bait and found himself in front of my fighter. I made a half roll and so did he. Both of us flew inverted for some time. At that moment I opened fire. A slight puff of smoke appeared in the area of the engine, aft of the cockpit, and the Sabre dropped toward the ground.

I saw well that it was an F-86 with black and white stripes. Two F-86 fighter wings were in Korea: one with yellow stripes, the other with black and white stripes. [Editor's note: the 4th FIW at Kimpo had black and white stripes early in the war, from November 1950. When the 51st FIW at Suwon became the second F-86 wing in the war, it introduced yellow bands. Later, these were adopted by all F-86 wings and the black and white stripes were discarded.]

While the fight continued, the 176th was fleeing for home.

The F-86 that had taken my hit began a forced landing. The 176th FAR's deputy commander, Sheberstov, landed at Antung before us and reported that he had shot down a Sabre. When we finished the battle and landed, I said that the 176th could not have shot down anything since they had seen no action.

Well, there was a scandal. There had been time to report this "great victory of Soviet aviation" to the Corps and to Moscow and that it was Sheberstov who had shot down the F-86 that had made an emergency landing. When the gun-camera films were studied, the Sabre was on my film, while on his film it was very tiny and could be observed against the coast line at a distance of more than a mile, or two to three kilometers. I was reassured by the division and Corps. They said, we will include it in your list and I thought, *What else can you do? Of course you will!*

I asked Sheberstov: "Of what color was the F-86 you shot down?" "With yellow stripes," answered he. Well, I thought, *We'll see which aircraft they find. If it has black and white stripes, then it's mine.* The black and white striped

Sabre was brought in.

After this disgrace Sheberstov, though he had claimed 14 kills, was not named a Hero of the Soviet Union. It is dangerous to lead the leadership, especially those in Moscow, into error and, besides, to be caught red-handed. Such things are not forgiven.

The F-86 pilot landed the aircraft skillfully. He turned out to be an ace pilot; his Sabre carried three rows of white stars, a total of 12 shot down aircraft. The pilot was immediately picked up by their Air Rescue Service, which was good, unlike ours. Two or three hours later, American strike aircraft came and started bombing and shooting up the area where the F-86 had landed. At that time the tide began rising, and water covered the landing area together with the Sabre. That night our technicians pulled it to the shore, moved it away for a considerable distance, and camouflaged it as a haystack. The next night, wings of the aircraft were cut off, and it was brought to Antung airfield. All of us had a chance to sit in the cockpit of this captured Sabre. The armament, instruments, flight and navigation equipment were those of the F-86A model.

Later, this valuable trophy was packaged in several containers and sent to Moscow. There, the Sabre was studied by various OKBs, with the purpose of improving our aircraft, particularly the MiG-15.

I succeeded in shooting down one radar-equipped F-94B. It happened during a daylight combat. There was a thick fog, the Americans had penetrated Chinese territory a distance of about 124mi (200km). I had words with Corps commander I. Belov on the air. I had been sitting with my group asking for clearance to take off. He did not give permission, waiting until the fog had lifted. He authorized the takeoff after the weather had become clear, and we nearly had let the enemy go. We took to the air, caught up with the F-94Bs, which were heading south, and attacked them. I shot down one aircraft of this type and afterward its wreckage was delivered to our airfield.

As to the training of the American pilots, I can say that the pilots of F-80s and F-86s were well trained. I do not agree with some of our men who say that we encountered inadequately-trained pilots who fled as soon as they saw our MiGs. American pilots had in general a higher

A meeting of Soviet pilot veterans of the Korean War.

standard of training as compared with ours, and, besides, the USAF pilots had more total flying hours. Many of these pilots had considerable combat experience from the Great Patriotic War.

We associated very little with the Chinese and Koreans. In January 1951, I was ordered to land in Mukden with pilots trained in night flying. We were stationed at Dunfyn then.

I landed with this squadron in Mukden and there I saw Chinese pilots. I talked with them in a mess room through an interpreter. They were sitting, each eating a plateful of borsch with rice. A local commander told me that their food had become rationed, as it was to the Russian pilots. The condition of the Chinese could be seen easily—emaciated, no adipose tissue at all, so thin and feeble. How could they withstand MiG-15 G-loads? The Chinese pilots sometimes lost consciousness in flight, not without reason.

Later I met Chinese pilots after they landed one or two regiments at Antung after they had received a severe mauling. The Chinese command asked us to train their pilots in tactics of air fighting against F-86s. I gave lessons twice explaining things on the blackboard, with fingers, and via an interpreter.

I think that Chinese pilots did not feel comfortable in the MiG-15 cockpit when they met Sabres or other American aircraft. It is very difficult to make a rated pilot within six months, as was wanted for combat actions with the Americans, especially if this pilot was poorly fed and had poor physical training. It is actually impossible, though our instructors tried to do their best so the Chinese could fight and survive.

If it was hard for us to fight against the Americans, what about the Chinese? Our Chinese allies were inadequately drilled for combat and suffered heavy losses. They were actually aerial targets for the Americans.

In our time, we tried to deploy North Korean pilots to one of the airfields in Korea. They landed there and were immediately destroyed by bombing, within one night. The next day all who had survived returned. I did not see them any more nor did I hear anything of them.

And now about aerial victory claims. I personally think that not all the aircraft claimed to have been shot down by both the Americans and our side were really killed.

In addition to gun cameras, we could determine whether an aircraft had fallen using information from our ground forces. The Americans' information was based on gun camera film and pilots' reports.

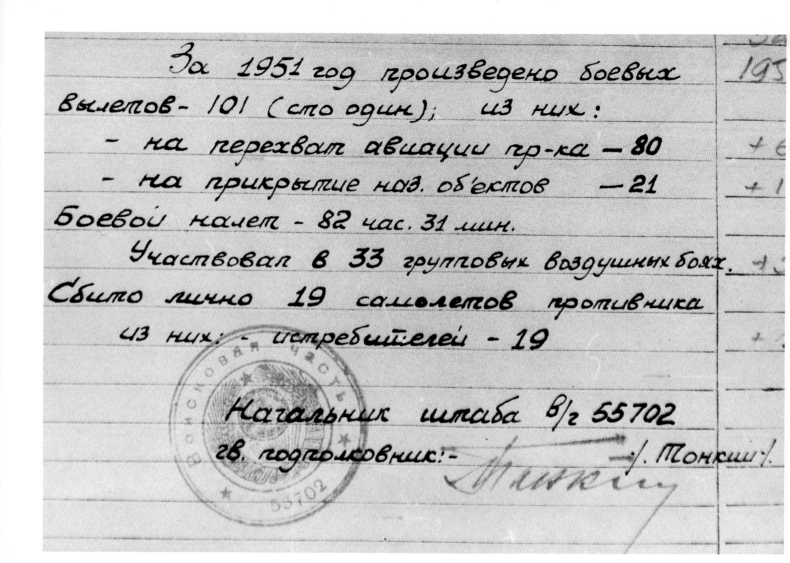

За 1951 год произведено боевых вылетов - 101 (сто один); из них:
  - на перехват авиации пр-ка - 80
  - на прикрытие наз. объектов - 21
Боевой налет - 82 час. 31 мин.
  Участвовал в 33 групповых воздушных боях.
Сбито лично 19 самолетов противника
из них: - истребителей - 19

  Начальник штаба в/ч 55702
гв. подполковник: -   /. Тонких /.

This page of Pepelyaev's flight log reveals his participation in the Korean War: "During 1951, 101 sorties were performed, among them 80 interception missions and 21 air support missions. Combat flying time—82hr, 31min. Participated in 33 group air combats. Shot down 19 enemy aircraft, all fighters."

Considering the low vulnerability of our MiG-15s to .50cal (12.7mm) fire, these claims were overstated. I believe that enemy pilots scored more kills than we did. This is partly because of the low proficiency of the Chinese and of our pilots who went into combat without proper practice, especially after our departure at the beginning of 1952.

I shot down 12 F-86s, six F-80s, four F-84s, and one F-94B, a total of 23 aircraft. Twenty were registered officially,

and I gave three to my wingman, A. Rozhkov. I thought he would be declared a Hero of the Soviet Union. But these kills did not help him: we buried him in Port Arthur.

The 196th FAR claimed to have destroyed a total of 104 enemy aircraft. We lost ten aircraft. Four pilots were killed, four were wounded. Two more aircraft and two pilots out of A. Blagoveshchenski's group, which was attached to our regiment, should be added to the above number.

The entire 324th FAD lost about 20 aircraft. The total number of enemy aircraft shot down by the 324th was 207 (including 103 kills by the 176th FAR). According to I. Kozhedub's data, the total number was 258. The ratio is approximately one to ten for all aircraft, of all classes and types.

Our regiment was more "lucky" to

shoot down fighters. Here are the data on the kills scored by the second squadron of the 196th FAR only: Maj. B. Bokach, six F-86s and one F-84; B. Abakumov, one B-29, three F-86s, and one F-94; Muraviev, four F-86s and one F-84 (he also shot down two Chinese MiG-15s by mistake); Nazarkin, two F-86s and one F-84; Pulko, two F-86s that collided during the pilot's attack and were counted as his kills; Litvinyuk, one F-94; and Vermin, one F-86.

Thus, 24 enemy aircraft were shot down, including 23 fighters and one bomber—one B-29, 16 F-86s, two F-84s, and four F-94s.

I recommended six pilots of my regiment for the title of Hero of the Soviet Union, but none were given this title.

My deputy, Col. A. Mitusov, shot down five aircraft in the Korean War. He had seen action during the Great Patriotic

War and had scored several kills there. Then, he had been put forward for the title of Hero, but it was not conferred. My deputy got into a temper, wounded the chief of supplies, who turned to be a rogue, and was sent to a penal battalion. Of course the recommendation was withdrawn.

I also recommended for the title squadron commander Maj. B. Bokach, flight commander Capt. V. Alfeev with eight kills, squadron deputy commander . Inanov who also claimed eight victories, B. Abakumov with his five kills, Capt. I. Zaplavnev who shot down six aircraft in Korea and six during the Great Patriotic War. None was awarded this title though earlier in the war the title was conferred for as few as four kills.

All of us were in correspondence with our families. Everything was as it always is in war: a field post office, censorship, and all. Our relatives knew where we were and what we did, but we were prohibited actually telling them. In our country, matters stand as follows: nobody knows anything formally, everything is secret, everything is a military or state secret, even the number of sheep tails, but everybody actually knows everything, and sometimes even things that are genuine secrets.

My wife knew where I was. In 1951 she was made very happy: she received an official envelope sent by post. She was shocked because the envelope was the kind used to inform loved ones of deaths of our pilots in Korea. But on this occasion, as it turned out, I. Kozhedub had decided to tell her about giving the rank of colonel to me before the appointed time. She swore that the rank did not matter to her if only her husband would return from the war.

We were continually propagandized that the American pilots killed, plundered, and violated the Koreans. Well, our task was to protect our brothers from the American bandits by gaining air superiority. Our main task was covering the railway across the Yalu River and the hydroelectric power plant; to perfect these tasks we should not have spared our health and our MiGs.

Each regiment had special departments and regimental deputy commander on politics (*zampolit*) that used to tell us such things as, "If you are taken prisoner, you will be deprived of everything." Ninety percent of my pilots had families in the USSR, and, naturally, none of them thought of defecting. We were not brought up to behave in this way. The idea of betraying our country could scarcely come to our heads. Neither $100,000 nor $1,000,000 could do anything in this case. As for me, I can say for sure that such thoughts did not occur to me; as for my colleagues...in any case, there was not a single deserter from the Soviet side during the entire period of the Korean war.

I was awarded two Orders of Lenin and was declared a Hero of the Soviet Union for my combat actions in the Korean War.

I. Kozhedub had recommended me for the second star of a Hero, but I was not given it. This recommendation was after we had left Korea and been replaced by other pilots who were inadequately trained. Our side began sustaining losses, American pilots began gaining the upper hand, and the upper strata chose to delay naming Heroes.

MiG-15 Versus F-86: Which Was Better?

Seldom in history did two fighters so similar in performance face each other in the air as during the three-year campaign between the Soviet MiG-15 and the American F-86 Sabre.

Both aircraft first flew in 1947, the MiG-15 at the end of December, the F-86 on 1 October. Both entered production in 1948, were manufactured by the thousand, and served the air forces of many countries. Numerous modifications of both aircraft were made. Both were built not only in their home countries but also in allied countries under license. The following is a comparison of the two aircraft:

The general arrangement of both fighters was similar. They were all-metal, single-seat monoplanes powered by a single turbojet with the wing swept back at 35deg and with swept tail surfaces.

The turbojet engines of both aircraft were installed in the rear fuselage and were circular in cross section. The MiG had an engine with a centrifugal compressor, the Sabre an axial compressor. In those versions fighting in Korea, MiG-15 and F-86 engines delivered approximately the same thrust. The MiG-15 had a higher thrust-to-weight ratio because of its lower weight.

The F-86 was a low-wing monoplane. The MiG-15 had a medium-set wing. The control system of Sabre used boosters while the MiG-15 had conventional controls. A reversible hydraulic booster was introduced into the aileron control of the MiG-15bis—cautiously, since there were cases of inadvertent entry into a spin before pilots got used to this system.

The F-86 had a torsion-box-type rigid wing, a structure that prevented wing dropping at any speed or altitude. The MiG-15 wing structure was the main cause of wing dropping: it was less rigid and was often built at plants that deviated from technical requirements. The MiG-15 had a higher wing thickness to chord ratio than the F-86, so the increased thrust of later Sabres gave them increased maximum speed as compared with the MiGs. For example, the MiG-15bis and F-86F had approximately equal thrust, but the speed of the MiG was 22mph (35km/h) lower.

F-86A and E versions had leading edge slats, which improved maneuverability. Designers of the F-86F-25 deleted the slats. The wing leading edge was extended 6in (152.4mm) at its root and 3in (76.2mm) at the wing tip (hence the term "6-3 wing"), which reduced thickness to chord ratio even more. This increased maximum speed by 6mph (10km/h).

Both fighters had swept empennage. The horizontal stabilizer of the MiG-15 was positioned at approximately mid-fin, while that of the F-86 was on the upper fuselage. The all-flying stabilizer was introduced on the F-86E version. This innovation was introduced to Soviet fighters only in 1955 with the MiG-19C.

No Sabres in the Korean War had afterburners, although water injection was introduced with the F-86E, increasing engine thrust. This way to increase thrust was not tried by the Soviets.

There was a striking difference in weapons. The MiG-15 was armed with a powerful battery of one 37mm and two 23mm guns. The rate of fire of the 37mm gun, handled by ordinary pilots, made it a marginal weapon against other fighters,

but the gun was effective agains bombers. Experienced pilots like E. Pe pelyaev think that the cannon battery when handled by them, was quite effec tive.

The Sabre had six .50cal (12.7mm machine guns (three on each side) with rate of fire of 110 rounds per second (rps and endurance of 15sec. The MiG-1! had the following rate of fire: N-37 gun 6–7rps; and two NR-23, 30rps. En durance was 15sec.

A positive factor for MiG-15 pilot was the MiG's high survivability when hi by .50cal (12.7mm) bullets. Sometime MiGs with up to 100 bullet holes wer repaired to fight again. F-86s also hac much resistance to 23mm projectile from the MiG but hits by 37mm projec tiles in even small quantities usually de stroyed the Sabre.

The gun sight was of great impor tance for both aircraft. The American had an automatic sight linked with rang ing radar. The Soviet pilot had to put th target into his ASP sight, estimate lea and range, and then fire. Besides, the AS often failed during high-G maneuverin so pilots used it as a simple collimatin sight. Working with this disadvantag demonstrates the high professionalism c Soviet pilots, who succeeded in shootin down Sabres during high-G combat.

The Sabre had good cockpit visibil ity. The pilot sat high and the canopy wa of single glass, without frames. In th MiG-15, the pilot sat deeply under smaller canopy shaped for better aerody namics and strength. This canopy was c two plates with a frame that degrade cockpit visibility. At first, water betwee the two plates froze at high altitudes mak ng the pilot practically blind to the rear, where he was usually attacked by Sabres. The ground technical staff had to blow air into the space between the two plates after almost every flight.

The MiG-15's ejection seat was reliable and no cases of pilot death caused by its failure were registered. But it had a considerable shortcoming. It could be activated only by the right hand. If this hand was injured in combat, the pilot had to reached across with his left hand, which was certain to lead to incorrect position during ejection and, as a consequence, injury.

The MiG-15 had a higher lift-to-drag ratio than that of Sabre (13.5 against 11; the "bis" had 14.6). But F-86 had less mid-fuselage cross section because of its axial-compressor engine. The F-86 picked up speed in dive quicker and recovered with less loss of altitude. Maximum speed of MiG-15 was 25mph (40km/h) less than that of F-86A. They had practically the same climb rate at sea level. The MiG was capable of higher rate of climb at altitude than Sabre because it had more thrust reserve. The MiG-15 had a climb-rate advantage beginning at approximately 20,000ft (6,000m), and the advantage increased with altitude.

All F-86 versions had better horizontal maneuverability because of their lower wing loading. The F-86's slats and the air brakes improved maneuverability in level flight significantly. The area of the air brake panels of the MiG-15 was evidently not enough. It was increased to some extent on the MiG-15bis, but was not enough as proven during combat in Korea. So MiG-15bis were built with air brake panels of still greater area beginning in 1952. Still, in this area, the MiG never reached the level of efficiency of the Sabre. This was considered when designing the MiG-17 and, to a greater extent, the MiG-17F, where the area of brake flaps was increased still further.

The Americans flew in anti-G suits, which resisted high Gs during combat. In the USSR, delivery of PPK-1 suits to VVS and PVO units commenced only after the war in Korea.

It is clear from brief analysis that the two aircraft were about equal when flown by experienced pilots. In air combat, much depended on tactics, experience, and the personal qualities of pilots. To sum up the above, the MiG-15 had al-

MiG-15

S-1—Prototype, first flight 30 December 1947.

MiG-15—Production fighter. First flight December 1948. *Engine:* RD-45F, rated at 5,005lb (2,270kg) thrust. *Armament:* one 37mm and two 23mm guns. *Sight:* ASP semi-automatic.

MiG-15bis (SD)—First flight in 1949. Series from 1950. Appeared in Korea in 1951. *Engine:* VK-1, rated at 5,952lb (2,700kg) thrust. Rate of climb and maximum speed increased from 652 to 668mph (1,050 to 1,076km/h). Hydraulic booster introduced in control system.

MiG-17—Fighter with VK-1A turbojet with afterburner rated at 5,952lb (2,700kg) thrust. Wing swept at 45deg with less thickness to chord ratio. First flight at the beginning of 1950. Did not participate in the Korean War. Maximum speed increased to 691mph (1,114km/h). Introduced into production in 1953, after Korean War.

UTI-MiG-15—Two seat trainer fighter with RD-45F engine. Test aircraft built in 1949. Production started in 1950.

MiG-15bisP (SP-1, SP-2, SP-5)—Interceptor prototypes equipped with radar sights. Prototypes built in 1949-50.

SB Lim-1, SB Lim-2, S-102, S-103—Licence versions of MiG-15 and MiG-15bis manufactured in Poland and Czechoslovakia.

F-86

XP-86—Prototype, first flight 1 October 1947.

F-86A—Production fighter. First flight 20 May 1948. *Engine:* J-47-GE-1, rated at 5,200lb (2,320kg) thrust. *Armament:* six .50cal (12.7mm) machine guns. *Sight:* automatic, with ranging radar.

F-86E—In series production from the end of 1950. *Engine:* J-47-GE-13 rated at 5,300lb (2,360kg). Rate of climb and maximum speed increased. All-flying tail (stabilizer) introduced.

F-86F—Engine rated at 6,128lb (2,780kg) thrust, new wing, with less thickness to chord ratio, without slats. Maneuverability at high altitude improved. Maximum speed increased. Rate of climb equal to MiG-15bis. Ten aircraft F-86F-2 and F-3 with four 20mm gun cannons sent to Korea, where they showed high efficiency.

F-86H—Multirole fighter. Engine rated at 9,304lb (4,220kg). Four 20mm guns. Introduced into production in 1953. Increased rate of climb. Ceiling increased to 50,064ft (15,500m). Maximum speed increased to 684mph (1,102km/h). Weight increased but horizontal maneuverability degraded.

TF-86F—Two-seat trainer fighter. Prototype manufactured in 1953. Two built.

F-86D and F-86L—Radar-equipped interceptor. Produced beginning in 1950. Engine with afterburner, rated at 7,326lb (3,340kg) thrust. Armament 24 2.75-in rockets in underfuselage container.

F-86K—Export version of F-86D with 4x20mm guns. Produced for allied countries. Versions of the Sabre were built in Australia, Canada, Italy, and Japan, most with other turbojets replacing J47s.

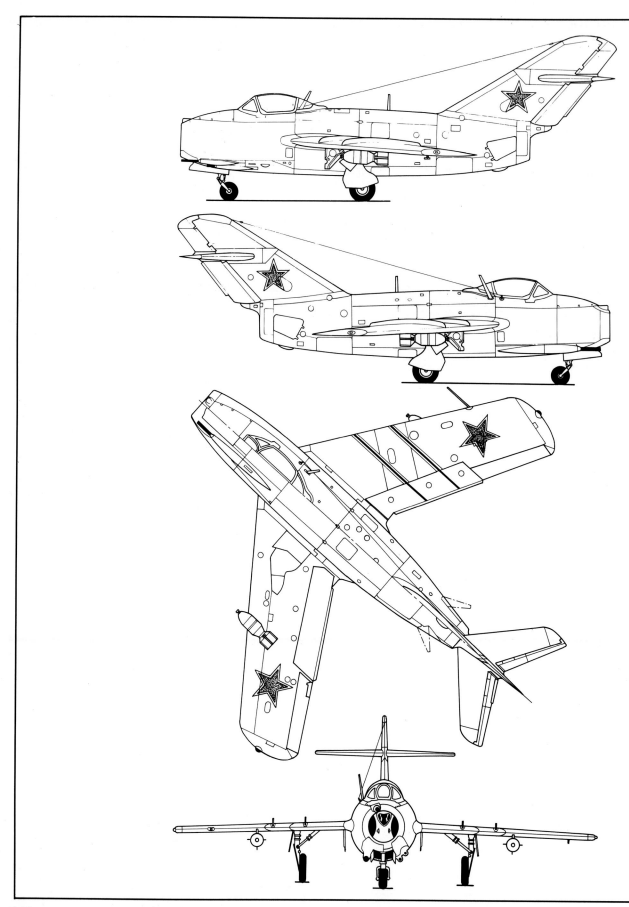

itude and climb superiority over the F-86. The Sabre outmaneuvered the MiG-15 in the horizontal plane.

The exposure of strong and weak sides of the aircraft determined the logic of combat. The MiG-15 tended to fight in the vertical and while climbing, the Sabre in the horizontal and while diving. In the vertical, the pilot of the MiG could control distance, using his better acceleration. Greater thrust permitted an aggressive approach toward the F-86 and an opportunity to break off by choice. But this advantage was canceled at low altitude.

Pilots of the MiG-15 sent to Korea did not have enough experience flying the MiG. Experience in the Yak-9, La-7, and other piston-engine aircraft left unsolved problems. The MiG's OSP-48 system was original, while night and IFR training was unusual for these pilots. Cockpit visibility was better as compared with piston-engine aircraft and powerplant operation was simpler and more reliable. This picture of the change to jets is completed with the high reliability and survivability of the MiG-15.

Soviet pilots, fighting in Korea, liked the aircraft for its simplicity of control and its survivability. The latter often meant life or death for the pilot.

The participation of MiG-15 and F-86 in the Korean War determined the future of fighter aircraft for many years. The MiG-21 and MiG-29 continued the So-

An early production series MiG-15bis equipped with the OSP-48 blind landing system and Bary IFF responder. The landing light is installed in the nose.

viet tendency toward simplicity and survivability, each becoming a sensation in the world of aviation in its time. In the West, the Sabre gave the way to the English Folland Gnat, the American F-104, the Northrop F-5, and, in the 1970s, the F-16.

Having gotten acquainted with the F-86, Soviet pilots made a number of suggestions to the Mikoyan OKB concerning the improvement of their MiG and its systems. American pilots did the same, seeking from industry new modifications of the Sabre which could outperform the MiG-15. The requirements of MiG pilots in Korea were the following:

• To equip the engine with afterburner for short-term and sharp increase of thrust for separation or to overtake an enemy. Such an engine was passing tests at that time, namely the VK-1F with afterburner thrust of 7,450lb (3,380kg), but production of MiG-17F with this engine started only when the war was over

• To increase the area of air brake panels. Work was undertaken but the problem was solved only with the MiG-17F

• To provide ranging radar, as on the Sabre. This feature was introduced in postwar period as the SRD-1 on the MiG-17 and MiG-19

• To introduce anti-G suits; PPK-1 suits were introduced only with the MiG-17

• To provide reliable mirrors for rearward visibility in combat. Soviet mirror, not yet perfect, underwent tests during the war. The authors have no knowledge of these periscopes in Korea. Production TS-27 periscopes were installed on the MiG-17

• To introduce a system of tail-section defense. The *Sirena* system was designed during the war and was installed

on some aircraft fighting in Korea at the end of war (according to Gen. G. Lobov). Later, this radar warning system became the standard equipment of all Soviet combat aircraft

• To improve the ejection seat, making it possible to eject using either hand. The new seat was introduced on the MiG-17

• To provide the pilot emergency and survival equipment in case of accident or of being shot down

• To improve cockpit visibility and to introduce a single-glass canopy without plates. Such canopies were being tested during the Korean War, and were introduced only on late MiG-17s

• To introduce camouflage appropriate to the color of the surrounding terrain. The MiG15bis with camouflage appropriate to the local landscape appeared in Korea in 1952. These aircraft successfully fought fighter-bombers, attacking them from below. But very soon after the war, camouflage was dropped because it reduced the aircraft's speed. Camouflage returned to Soviet combat aviation for the second time after the destruction of Arab aircraft on the ground at airfields during the 1967 Six-Day War. After that, Soviet aircraft were painted almost within days

• To introduce additional armor. Production of the MiG15bis with additional armor was started in 1952

• To provide pilots with protective helmets. These began to be introduced in the VVS in the late 1950s

This list could be continued. But as it shows, the Soviet aircraft industry was strongly influenced by the Korean War, and completed many improvements, most introduced only after the war.

Both sides sought to acquire examples of the enemy's fighter aircraft by any technique that would work.

Index